CW00925434

A Prose Miscellany

KEITH DOUGLAS

A Prose Miscellany

As a child he was a militarist . . .

COMPILED & INTRODUCED
BY
Desmond Graham

CARCANET

First published in Great Britain in 1985 by
Carcanet Press Ltd
208–212 Corn Exchange Buildings
Manchester M4 3BQ

The publishers acknowledge the financial assistance of
the Arts Council of Great Britain

Douglas, Keith
  A prose miscellany.
  I. Title   II. Graham, Desmond
  828'.91208   PR6054.0836

  ISBN 0-85635-526-7

Typeset by Paragon Photoset, Aylesbury
Printed in England by Short Run Press, Exeter

Contents

Acknowledgements   6

Introduction   7

Douglas at Christ's Hospital: 1932–38   13

Correspondence with Edmund Blunden 1939–40   38

Excerpts from *Augury*   42

Contributions to *The Cherwell*   45

Correspondence 1940–41   68

Correspondence 1941–42   77

Draft of *Alamein to Zem Zem*   98

Correspondence 1943   115

'Death of a Horse'   137

'The Little Red Mouth'   139

'Giuseppe'   141

Correspondence 1944   144

Sources   156

Acknowledgements

I should like to thank holders of copyright material printed here: J. C. Hall, Douglas's executor, for material by Douglas and himself; Mrs Claire Blunden; Shakuntala Tambimuttu, and Tambimuttu's Literary Executor, Jane Williams; and Mrs T.S. Eliot. For providing material in private hands, I thank J.C. Hall and Mrs T.S. Eliot. I should like to acknowledge, with gratitude for MS material from their archives which is reprinted here, the assistance of the following libraries: The British Library; the Brotherton Collection, The Brotherton Library, Leeds University; The Harry Ransom Humanities Research Center, The University of Texas at Austin. Material from Douglas's *Complete Poems* is used by kind permission of Oxford University Press © 1978. I thank the Research Committee of the University of Newcastle upon Tyne for funds enabling me to consult MSS.

I should like to thank Jenny Stratford for putting at my disposal many years ago the Douglas letters she had found, and working on them with me. For support over many years, I should like to thank J.C. Hall, whose exceptional generosity was again shown to me over the copyright material printed here. I am grateful to Mrs Claire Blunden for similar generosity. I should like to thank Robyn Marsack of Carcanet Press, for transcribing MSS, for continuing editorial assistance and for the imaginative understanding with which she saw, and gave to me, the shape of this book. I should like to thank Trude Schwab for sharing every aspect of the book's making. Alison Forster, Kathleen O'Rawe and Doris Palgrave deserve thanks for their lively secretarial help, Katherine Graham for a finely judged 'going away', Daniel Brint for the missing piece of the jigsaw, and Dr. R. S. White for a conversation which conceived the whole book. With Douglas's name on the title page, this book is not mine to dedicate. As it is a book about the creative participation through which literature is made, however, that part which is mine I should like to dedicate to Catharine Carver, for her example of how that creative participation works.

Introduction

This book is more than a miscellany. It is a portrait of Douglas in his own words; a story of pre-war childhood, wartime Oxford, service in the Middle East, experience of the desert fighting of 1942–43, and the preparations for the Normandy landings. It is also the story of a writer's development, from outstandingly precocious beginnings through to the writing of the war poems and narrative on which his reputation now firmly rests; the story of a literary friendship between Edmund Blunden and Keith Douglas, a poet of the First World War and one of the Second; and the story of how, pressed by the hazards of wartime and the conviction that he will not survive, a writer works towards the preservation of his work through publication.

Douglas's *Complete Poems* were published in 1978; a new edition of *Alamein to Zem Zem* in 1979; the present editor's biography, *Keith Douglas 1920–1944*, in 1974. This book is therefore a miscellany in its determination not to overlap with the two previously published volumes, and in being based largely on work which has emerged since the biography. That new work includes the full correspondence with Blunden, found by Jenny Stratford among the Blunden papers at Texas; Douglas's letters to Tambimuttu of 'Editions Poetry (London)', concerning publication of his work, in 1944; and an extensive but abandoned draft, revising part of *Alamein to Zem Zem*, made by Douglas around September 1943. This was found, like the letters to Tambimuttu, among 'Poetry (London)' papers rescued for Mrs Douglas by J.C. Hall, after the bankruptcy of the publisher. The differences between this revision of *Alamein*, made before military and other forms of censorship intervened, and the extant published version, are outlined in the Sources at the end of this book. Other recently discovered material includes an uncollected school poem, an early draft of 'Vergissmeinnicht', and essays and stories from school exercise books.

The book is not a miscellany in that it includes all that survives

of both sides of Douglas's literary correspondence — with
Blunden, T.S. Eliot, J.C. Hall and Tambimuttu. It also includes all
the stories and virtually all the prose Douglas published at school
and Oxford; the only two of his Middle East stories to survive —
one of them published here for the first time; his important essay
'Poets in This War' and the other, occasional, prose that happened to survive his various travels between 1941 and 1944. The
elements of incompleteness in this material, however, are part of
the story. The gaps are the gaps which time and especially wartime bring about in our contact with the past: the losses of work,
written and unwritten, which the circumstances of war enforce,
and against which Douglas pitched his efforts and, through the
help of others, succeeded largely in overcoming. The continuing
thread is Douglas's own view of himself and the world: the view
of one who, as he declared in the opening words of the first story
of this book, as a child was a militarist.

As a child Douglas was so; and, as the letters and poems show,
the part of him which was a child remained so — militant, active,
delighting in adventure and seeking simplicity. The growing
man knew, and at El Alamein had confirmed for him, that it was
only the child who could be militarist. Against what pleased the
fantasy, what enabled him to enter with ceaseless curiosity the
world of a tank regiment in action, was another view. That view
was there from the start in what Blunden observed as Douglas's
way of seeing things 'with a remarkable keenness'. A keenness
which had led Douglas, at the age of six to gaze impassively at the
needle entering his arm, after his mother had advised him that
he need not look at the injection. In that first autobiographical
story, which Mrs Douglas recalled coming across when Douglas
returned to school after a holiday when he was twelve, that
keenness is there in the portrait of the father he had not seen since
the age of six, the awareness of disappointed childish energies,
the final focusing upon his mother and the event which was to
lead to the break-up of his family home.

Between that story and the widely published Oxford poet, is
the sixteen-year-old writer who, for a school exercise, could
demonstrate that a poem of his was composed with a network of
submerged allusions, a mastery of prosody; and could affirm,
with conviction, that the poem was nonetheless spontaneously
created; and the writer of the same age, effortlessly and cunningly, weaving into his essays and stories memories of a visit to
Gorizia, quotations from his own writing, and delicately per-

ceived memories of his childhood. Already, at sixteen, Douglas had found words for the desire which lay behind so much of his writing: 'I hope that some of the earlier experiences may shake out into a perspective in which I may look at them unemotionally' ('November'). His writing, to the end, was a shaking out, as confident hands shake out soil through a sieve; and for his implement he used the strictest of verse forms, the most formally articulated prose. These forms became his perspective, a means to detachment: and through them emerges experience far from unemotional.

But Douglas wrote also for the sheer pleasure of it. Much that is here delights through its humour, its sense of ironies, its capacity to capture incident and character in image or phrase. Almost everything he wrote — and I would exclude a piece from *Citadel*, printed here because I suspect it was an extended exercise in filling a maximum of space with a minimum of substance — carried the impress of his vitality of mind. Except by design, he could not be boring. His matter, however, is determined by the occasion, the whim of his moods and the circumstances in which he lived. The Oxford poet turns into the spokesman for youth against age, sense against cant, a castigator of 'adult' oppression and the militarism with which it has confronted a younger generation. In turn he becomes the poet in the Forces eager, then anxious and then desperate, to see his work gathered into a collection before he leaves for the Middle East. Arrived there he is the visitor, one who fluctuates between enthusiasm for what he sees and anger at exclusion, and who knows he has been sent to take part in battle. Having been placed in a backwater by the military authorities and forgotten there, Douglas drove himself to the battle of El Alamein, in direct defiance of orders. For what he met we have his own account in the fragment of the narrative and in the poems he sent back to Britain. In the fragment there is still the buoyant, self-aware curiosity, moving step by step towards the realities of war which previously had lived only in the imagination. In the poems there is a focusing of detachment upon that experienced by the soldier himself: his distance from what he does and the damnation which that distance reveals.

Douglas's confidence in re-shaping his art so as to convey truly his experience of war, comes across above all in his letters to J.C. Hall. It is unjust that through them Hall should appear as one who failed to appreciate these poems, for Hall has long been a staunch supporter of Douglas's entire work. In the context of their correspondence, however, the injustice is alleviated by other discoveries: that it was Douglas's appreciation of Hall's help that led him to articulate the terms of the art he had found; that without Hall's support, as Douglas acknowledged, many of the poems would never have been written. A similar situation arises in Douglas's dealings with Tambimuttu. From the outset Douglas had misgivings about Tambi's efficiency and taste. In England in 1944 he was driven to desperation by his delays. But Tambi's support was crucial. As is shown here, Tambi could rightly claim to have 'discovered' Douglas, and it was his discovery which gave Douglas the prospect of publication so valuable to his work in 1943–44. It is by contrast with the creative contribution of Hall and Tambimuttu that T.S. Eliot's part appears so unhelpful. Blunden's was on an entirely different level.

Blunden is widely known to have been one who took an extraordinarily personal and long-lasting care over those who studied under him at Merton. With Douglas, moreover, he shared something vital to himself and important to Douglas — memories of being a pupil at Christ's Hospital, the school of Coleridge, Lamb and Leigh Hunt. By September 1939, Blunden shared something else: the knowledge that Douglas's generation was to face the destruction of war which lived almost daily in his memory, through recollections of the Somme and Paschaendaele. Douglas, who had received his kindly support as Oxford poet, was to become his successor as poet and chronicler of war: an emphasis Blunden quietly reiterated in his letters to him, deftly placing it to deflect from his recognition of the kind of price which he knew to be involved. For Blunden, in these letters so completely pacific, so supportively holding back from expressing the anguish he felt, was confronted in Douglas with someone who actively sought out war, was impetuous and disquietingly reckless; someone who, in his correspondence, was frank to the point of brashness and a resolute displayer of himself. Blunden was undeterred. With a truly creative modesty, he maintained his civil discourse, praised and encouraged, and when he felt at odds with what he read he covered his candour with protestations of being old-fashioned, out-of-date. Douglas nowhere shows any concern for Blunden's own writing — though his shaping of *Alamein* may well have been helped by the precedent of Blunden's *Undertones of War* with its appendix of poems. Yet his pique when no news from Blunden arrives suggests how much unspoken care was felt. Douglas sends Blunden his poems, even while he has other potential outlets. The correspondence is sustained through to Douglas's departure from the Middle East in November 1943. They did not meet in England in 1944. Mrs Douglas has suggested that Douglas might have felt complicated about Blunden's altered domestic situation — he was in the process of re-marrying; perhaps Douglas waited for Blunden to contact him? Whatever the reason it seems probable that their failure to meet deeply affected Blunden. Blunden's care and his own complex feelings about the relationship are unmistakable in an as yet unpublished piece, kindly shown to me by his biographer, Barry Webb. There Blunden's awareness of the edges of Douglas's character is in no doubt, and neither is the feeling that perhaps he was himself being surpassed. Nothing of this is given away in the letters.

The other presence in this book is Douglas's mother. After her vital part in the very first story she is there only as the link between Douglas and his various correspondents. Yet that is an important and, perhaps, a surprising role. Though she had no literary expertise or experience, Douglas is happy to use her as a kind of agent. Editors and publishers defer to her judgement. Had her side of their correspondence been thought worthy of preservation, we might well have seen the strength of her role. But this too is a significant gap. Mrs Douglas always under-estimated her part in her son's creative work. Her illness, *encephalitis lethargica*, sleepy sickness, for years left her too debilitated to give much help; her constant moves from lodging to lodging or friend's house to friend's house during summer holidays — sub-letting her furnished bungalow to supplement a meagre income — gave no secure home. These things she emphasized in conversation with me. A different emphasis has come to my thinking since her death in 1981, and with increasing strength: the quality of her mind, her own keenness of sight. A brief passage from a letter she wrote to John Baber (the husband of Jocelyn Baber, to whom Douglas defended aspects of *Alamein to Zem Zem*, p.153) on 20 July 1944, six weeks after Douglas's death, in its precise phrasing and its assertion of selfhood will perhaps show how much she had in common with her son. Douglas had spent his last Christmas with the Babers — his mother lived as housekeeper/companion there — and it was partly out of gratitude for that holiday that she spelt out her feelings to them.

My first reaction to the news of Keith's death was one of almost terror of the empty future and the knowledge that the last person to whom I mattered was gone for ever. It is queer to feel that no one — however long you live — will ever mind again if you are there or not — will ever in fact need you *personally*, again. . . . Fate, it seems, grudged me even [him] — but not even fate can take away the memory of him and of the things he wanted me to do if he passed on leaving them still unfulfilled. Only a total blackout could do that — and then what is 'I' would no longer be there to matter.

An Untitled Autobiographical Story
(c. 1932)

As a child he was a militarist, and like many of his warlike elders, built up heroic opinions upon little information, some scrappy war stories of his father. Most of the time he was down in the field, busy, with an absurdly puposeful look on his round face, about a tent made of an old sheet, and signposted with a board saying 'sergeants' mess'. He was quite at home there for hours, while he was four and five, telling himself stories as he ran about, and sometimes stopping a moment to contemplate the calf who shared that field, a normally quiet animal, but given to jumping five-barred gates. As you would expect, he played with lead soldiers, and toy artillery, and was most fond of the cavalry and the highlanders. Unlike the other troops who either marched sedately with sloped arms or sat bolt upright on their caracoling steeds, the highlanders were charging, their kilts flying at a swift angle out behind them and the plumes upon their heads also flying out, though often in the wrong direction for the broken heads were fixed back on with matches, and swivelled easily.

His father did not spend very much time with him, but would speak to him of war and boxing and shew the boy his great muscles, for here at least he could shew them off to unbounded admiration. He teased his son, and pinched and tormented him sometimes, but Keir liked his father better than his mother, who fondled him a deal too much and cried sometimes, even then Keir and Billy Cameron who lived near, were often about together in trees. They built a house once, in the big tree at the end of Billy's garden, but Billy fell out of it. So they were kept away from there and played in the garden itself. Captain Cameron entertained them with a service revolver and a bomb, but in the end they were left to themselves.

'My father,' said Billy, 'shot a German point blank. He saw him coming out of a pillbox and shot him before the German could shoot Daddy.' Keir was a little annoyed that Billy should tell this story, condensed though it had become, so often. But point blank

was admittedly a good thing to say and in return he explained
how his own father was shot by a Turk.

'*My* father wouldn't have let a measly old Turk shoot him,' said
Billy and Keir's reposte was squashed. Yet he was very proud of
his father and went home to his supper sadly down the road past
Miss Drivers, and Colonel Transome, the old man who was so
funny because he never wore a waistcoat, and Miss Peck and Mr
Peck who made cider, and each of the other neighbours whom
Keir pictured not by remembering their faces, but the colour of
their front hedges and fences. He reached up and opened his
own front door, which had a high knob. His father was inside,
taking off his shoes, in a good temper. 'Hallo, Old Bean,' he said
'been climbing trees?' Keir beamed. He loved to be called Old
Bean. 'Hallo dadda, Captain Cameron threw a bomb at me.' 'Oh,
you didn't mind though did you? You're a tough guy.' 'Gee whiz
I'm a tough guy, Daddy, tell me about Yukon Jake again.'
Captain McDonald raised a chair in one hand and shook it. He
recited ferociously

> Yukon Jake
> was as tough as a stake,
> hardboiled as a picnic egg.
> He combed his hair
> with the leg of a chair
> and drank his beer by the keg.

Keir repeated it furiously and with great pleasure. 'Now teach
me to box' he said. He was not restrained from punching his
father's amateur-champion broken nose by the entry of his
grandfather, Mr Castellain, a courteous and courtly old gentleman who now spent his life playing patience. Mr C. received the
bomb story less enthusiastically. He had once been in the volun-
teers, but had never fought anyone in his life. Harrow and Balliol
and an addiction to natural history and good manners had made
him a quiet spoken and kindly old man. Considerate and un-
selfish to his own class but almost unaware of the existence of any
other.

The smell of his supper, which was a kind of broth prepared by
his grandmother attracted Keir into the other room. 'Where's
Mummy?' he asked Mrs Castellain. 'She went down to the
village, dear, to do some shopping. Now go and wash your
hands before you eat your supper. There's a good boy.' Probably
that type of phrase annoys every child. It galled Keir, anyway,

and he said pettishly 'Don't want to wash my hands. They're quite clean. I want my supper.' 'Now don't be rude to Granny. Go and wash.' 'I won't wash my hands —' Keir was beginning when his father came in and told him angrily to hurry up and go, and Keir went.

When he was coming downstairs he heard his mother come in through the front door. She looked pretty but tired out, and smiled at Keir who was a consolation to her for many things. 'I'm going to eat my supper Mummy.' 'All right dear, I'll come and watch you.'

Keir ate his supper, and talked a good deal, in spite of the reprimands of his grandmother, who still thought that little boys should be seen and not heard, and often said so. Outside the evening sunlight reminded Keir of fairies, for it did indeed endue the garden with a dreamlike quality. So he demanded a story from his grandfather, who was in the drawing room playing with cards.

'Very well, little man, I'll tell you a story in one minute, when I've finished this game of patience,' said his grandfather, in his curious calm voice which held no trace of foreign accent though its polite unruffled tones themselves must have come over the channel with his own grandfather, escaping the revolution by the aid of servants to whom he, luckily, had been kind.

Keir waited two minutes before he asked for his story again, and received the same answer, out of the corner of his grandfather's mouth, as the card game, for long the most exciting part of the old gentleman's life, drew to its most exciting moment and completion. The minutes continued to drag slowly by, and at last, Keir realised that he would soon be hauled storyless to bed. When he had asked once more and received the same unhurrying answer, he suddenly grew furious, and overturned the old gentleman's precious ricketty table.

Mr Castellain had never been so near anger in twenty years. But after Keir's simple explanation that he wanted his story, he said kindly, 'You're sorry you turned my table over, aren't you, little man?' And on Keir's admission of penitence (for he saw that would begin his story soonest) the story was begun.

In the morning Keir was woken by the sun and the birds and lay in bed listening to them and thinking to himself, until it occurred to him that people were about in the house and his mother's and father's beds were empty. He went and peered out, and saw through the bannisters a group of people standing in the hall, about his mother, who lay asleep on a stretcher or as it seemed to Keir a funny sort of bed. He realised almost at once that his mother was ill and ran downstairs on his bare feet asking what was the matter with her, as they took her away out of the front door. Someone he had never seen took him back to his bed with some unsatisfying explanation, and locked the door on him. He began immediately to scream and beat upon it, but they had all gone and he was alone, locked in. He became frantic, fell on the floor and shouted curses he had heard 'Curse damn bother darn bloody' in a string as long as he could put together, until he got up from the floor and hit his head on the door knob. It hurt and with some idea of punishing the door knob he hit his head on it five or six times more, very hard, and then subsided on the bed sobbing.

In a few minutes his grandfather came up and succeeded in calming him, explaining that his mother had an illness, called Sleepy Sickness, but she would be well soon, when she had gone to the Hospital and had a rest. With that, for the moment, Keir was content.

from *An Unfinished Autobiographical Fragment*
with the Epigraph: *'O spires O streams . . .'*
(1937)

When he was four, his mother had been very ill. He never sensed anything wrong when she came back from hospital; and when his father, a hearty playmate whom he secretly feared and wholeheartedly admired, disappeared and Olwen too, he wept as much as his mother.

It was soon apparent that lack of a father meant lack of money, and after a curtailed prep-school career, Peter entered Christ's Hospital where, being somewhat old for his age, he had attained a certain seniority by his fifteenth year.

He was now, at the age of fourteen, tall (some five feet nine inches), and fair, with very white skin and large brown eyes, long-lashed. He sat now sprawled on a stone seat, whose white stone shone back the sun at him disconcertingly. Sunlight, the blue glare of sky and far off cricketing sounds mingled, coming gently to his notice through eyes half shut and dreamy ears, moving him to an indescribable feeling of melancholy and long-ing, which both compelled and denied analysis. He began stumbling in his mind after this ignis fatuus discontent, this definite and indescribable disquiet, and suddenly caught up with it: suddenly knew that it was a desire to share beauty, the pleasantness of this summer afternoon, with someone else, someone to understand not this only, but every tossed thought and ambition. This would be a girl evidently: he pictured her for many days after that.

Walking along Eastbourne front in the holidays, he looked carefully at the faces of the girls who passed him. Some, freckled and pleasant, attracted him instantly: any one of these might have been his sympathiser, and he turned heavily into the belonged to an acquaintance. The pleasant artificial smell of the baths dispelled his gloom immediately. He changed quickly and climbed to the highest diving board. Here he stood rigid with muscles braced, yet trying to look as though each sinew stood thus in his body always. Two old women on the balcony regarded him with obvious admiration and whispered comments. Below him a hirsute out-of-condition young man leaned smoking against a pillar and shook ash into the bath. He was not interested in divers; his piggy eyes were turned with X-ray interest upon the charms of the baths attendant. Peter dived. He kept his body scrupulously straight, looking down upon the water as the air sang past him. Only a sideways wriggle in the air enabled him to avoid the underwater swimmer who broke surface suddenly beneath him, and he swam painfully to the rail smarting from flat impact with the water. The underwater swimmer followed him. She was small [. . .]

❦

From 1931–1938 Douglas was at Christ's Hospital. A keen rugby player and swimmer, a dedicated horseman, a resolute opponent of authority and the injustices of boarding school life, a devoted member of the school's O.T.C., a generally admired artist, it was as a writer that his reputation was most firmly based. From December 1934 he was a main contributor of poems, essays and stories to the school's thrice yearly literary magazine *The Outlook*. By the time he left, his poems had been taken by *Bolero* (an Oxford magazine), the annual *The Best Poems of 1939*, the *Sussex County Magazine* and *New Verse*. One of his school contemporaries regarded his talent highly enough to retain classroom essays Douglas had discarded, as did a master.

H. R. Hornsby retrieved from a wastepaper basket and kept for thirty years exercise books Douglas had thrown there. Some of the pieces which follow survived through their foresight.

●

Strange Gardener
(School Exercise Book; 'English 24.1.36')

Over the meadows,
framed in the quiet osiers, dreams the pond,
region of summer gnat-busyness,
where, in the afternoon's blue drowsiness,
fish plop among the water-shadows:
and the cool trees wait beyond.

A young man dwelt there,
with a swift, sad face, and full of phantasy,
repeating, as he heard it,
the alliterative speech of the water-spirit;
smoothing his pale hair
with automatic ecstasy.

This was his garden,
uncultivated, (order hated him)
whence, in a winter-madness,
(whose scourge filled him with recklessness,
seeing the frost harden),
the water-spirit translated him.

Explanation

A   Scheme

(i) I have not kept very strictly to any metre, but the metre is, roughly:

```
- u u - -
u - u - u - u - u -
u - u - u - u
- - - u u - u u
u - u - u - u -
```

(ii) The scheme of rhyming is:

A
B
C
C   last syllable only rhyming
A
B

B   Meaning

Over the meadows . . . *cf. Frederick Prokosch*	The first line is intended to take the reader well away from his surroundings immediately.
framed . . .	you are a rook flying over the pond, and looking down at it.
the quiet osiers . . . *cf. F.P.*	you are a rook, flying over the pond, and looking rustling is inaudible, you are not distracted from the important thing, the pond.
gnat-busyness . . .	this is not, of course, a spelling mistake, but quite a different word from business.
fish plop among the water-shadows . . .	you have flown over the meadows as a bird. Now you are a water-being, hanging over the pond in the summer.
trees *wait* beyond . . .	these did not distract you from your contemplation of the pond, but they are there for you, when you are ready, to look at them.
a swift, sad face . . . *the main idea of this verse is taken from the chief charcter of 'The Star-born'*	the swiftness of his face is in the lines of it, his high cheek-bones and the curved hang of his hair. It is his eyes that are sad, because his thoughts are more beautiful than reality.
repeating . . . the alliterative speech . . . *this idea also from 'The S-b'*	he repeats it, struck with its beauty, as a child will repeat what is said to it.
alliterative . . .	the speech of water is an interminable cavalcade of similar sounds.
automatic ecstasy . . . *his pale hair . . . C. Day Lewis in 'From Feathers to Iron' speaks of 'tow-headed poets'*	he is not aware of his action, but the feel of his hair, soft and smooth under his hand, gives him pleasure. Cf. T. S. Eliot 'she smooths her hair with automatic hand'.
a winter madness . . . seeing the frost harden . . . *this has some connection with 'The Tempest' 'Doth suffer a sea-change' cf. 'translated'*	The sight of the beauty of summer dying all about him caused him such acute misery that he was temporarily mad.
the water-spirit translated him . . .	i.e. he drowned himself in the throes of his despondent insanity. For the water-spirit cf. Henry Williamson 'The Star-born'.

General

This explanation is intended to shew that although the main

idea of the poem was spontaneous, and the poem itself is short, the scheme behind it is lengthily and carefully thought out. The lapses in metre are put in purposely, in an attempt to make it less stereotyped and more interesting.

Fragment — Death of the Squire
(OUTLOOK, March 1937)

And in a great house not far from the labourer's cottage, the fourth old man looks out of his window at the wind-bent trees and the fields stretching away to the dark wood on the hill's brow.

Brown dots move over the fields, matching the bare woods, and red coats gleam in the austere sunshine. To the ears of his imagination comes clearly the eternal note of the hunting horn, and the pain of that is more than the pain of the other old men. For this one is a poet: and where the others feel dolefulness or annoyance, he understands the full meaning of every movement of earth and condition of mind and body. Now that the hunt is gone over the hill, he still looks out on his inheritance. In the fire a log falls, and he turns suddenly with a curse, mumbled into a coughing fit. . . .

He shall rise up at the voice of the bird . . .
And the grasshopper shall be a burden.

In the fire are faces, faces first comical, then familiar; old companions caricatured, sharers of good runs, out on the hill there. He turns, looking at the hilltop again, and stumbles out of the room. Hatless, coatless, without even a stick, he walks determined to reach the wood, where he will find his friends, all waiting, so glad to see him.

As he plods, with difficulty negotiating stiles and gates, he thinks of the reunion, making in his mind a list of those waiting in the dark walks of the wood. At his entry, a rabbit scuttles in the underbrush to his left, and he is amazed at the sharpness of his hearing, lost for many years, now come again. So quick now his ears, that he can easily hear the piping, though it is evidently far away among the thin trunks of trees and brown leaf-piles where the partridges hide. He has no doubt of his direction, but walks more firmly always, over the crackling leaves, and the wood grows darker, full of the noises he loves.

The piping sounds clearer now to him, like a penny whistle in tone, yet playing a music unattained by the greatest composer. There is a rustling all round him, all moving among the trees towards the music, and he goes at a good round pace, stepping high over obstacles. Here at the top of the hill is the wood's heart, and here the trees thin out to a circle wide enough for dancing. The old man walks agilely into the gathering: they are all here, and the Piper sits traditionally, cross-legged, and perpetually playing, without breath-pauses: and he has in his ancient eyes all wisdom and all youth. The old man sits before him and looks up, wondering how such a face ever frightened those who saw it. In a minute he will greet his friends, who crowd about him: but first he must rest, and the music so close to him calls him irresistibly to sleep. . . .

November
(OUTLOOK, December 1936)

Drying in the sun on summer beaches, my mind achieves that almost impossible state, 'thinking of nothing.' I watch the far-off smoke-trails, or the precise curveting of seagulls, finding in these things a contentment which is above analysis. Always among familiar companions and continual occupations my summer days pass too quickly, for boredom may be washed off like dirt in the warm sea; and who may think dismally, watching the form of downland take shape under a lucky brush?

But as the days grow shorter, I must think more and more of past summers, chance friends who were very pleasant companions on those sunny days; and who are now passed, with such summers, into oblivion, whence only memory recalls them.

I hope that some of the earlier experiences may shake out at last into a perspective in which I may look at them unemotionally, deriving a pleasure from the contemplation of them not mixed with nostalgia. But now; old photographs, allusions, the faces of strangers, a thousand chances bring before me with sudden vividness people and incidents not thought of for some years. Drowsing pleasantly through mathematics, grown meaningless by repetition, I stumble suddenly into the woods by the old church of St Martha at Guildford, whose Sunday afternoon peace is disturbed by treble battle-cries.

Fircones hurtle among the tall tree trunks, and I, an ammunition-carrier, make my way down a side-path, hotly pursued by enemies whose supply is exhausted. So swiftly that I cannot follow the connection, prep.-school days fade, and I am in a field on a colder afternoon. Ringed about with my breath, I am led forward to meet my new pony, who is too tall for me. I am given a sugar-lump, which I hold out to him with friendly directness. He knocks me down. Only the sound of my name recalls me from these voyages among 'those quaint and charming islands of our childhood.'

It is for these reminiscences that I dread my November days; the fireside reverie is too productive of them. And yet how pleasant in these colder days is the exertion of running, tedious in summer; how welcome the occasional warm days recalling summer, and the fire and buttered toast on colder days.

The woods and hedgerows wear colours as beautiful as those of summer, though more austere; and the leaf carpets are well fitted to walk over. November is the best month of the year in the woods, when autumn is almost complete, winter well started.

Christmas in the distance is there to comfort the gloomiest longing for summer; and books, neglected these four months past for tennis-courts and sparkling water, are there waiting. The old books, read and re-read, liked for many seasons, come into their own again.

In other countries, under a sky perennially blue, I shall never pine to 'be in England, now that April's there,' but neither the straw-jacketed wine-bottles of Italy nor the clear depth of South Sea waters, nor any attraction of mere exoticism, shall compensate me for November lost.

Reading
(School exercise book; 'English Essay/Sept. 1937')

There are, I know, some who can read any book, swiftly skimming over the pages an almost photographic eye, and recording their impressions in notebooks. Again, there are those who live in perpetual happiness among a few books. No cover, lurid though it be and clever, or quiet and sympathetic, can persuade them to read a new book. No review, glowing with unaccustomed praises, can wake in them any desire to know more of the reviewer's choice. Nothing will suffice, but that they should read the old books over and over again. Moreover, there are those to whom any cover stiffer than paper is as a seal. I am not, as a reader, to be classed with any of these. Nor do I claim, as might naturally be expected after this denial, to have found the happy mean of these three attitudes.

In my reading, books are of three categories; the books I set out to read, the books I ought to read, and the delightful books of which I read parts by accident.

As for the books I set out to read, they are of many sorts, according with my mood or my surroundings. After a bout of intellectual reading, I fly back, like the prodigal, to the direct, unassuming writing, to sail hot seas in an open boat, with a cup of water a day, or fight beside my ancestor 'the gude Sir James', striking immortal blows in defence of Bruce's heart. Sometimes I swim through poetry like a trout in summer water, nibbling a little here or there, with the fine long words sliding across my brain as the trout feels currents pass him. Sometimes I am brought up short by some unearthly play of words, and spend a few melancholy minutes trying to trace such magic to its source.

No cudgelling will make my brain take notice of the books I ought to read. Hot fingers comb and recomb my hair into the same disorder, and my mind seizes eagerly at every chance illusion, flying away from the strict subject over far fields of imagination.

Finally there are the books which I find by accident, each bringing me a little isolated picture. In this way I found Kebriones lying with his skull smashed; I saw a lion chasing St Jerome's monks helter-skelter down their cloister; and I met Lord George Hell, stepping out of Mr Aeneas' shop with his saintly mask cunningly fitted. Just as I go to a new place always with the thought of what friends I shall make, how I shall speak wonderingly to them of 'last year, when I did not know you;' so I can never go among books without this pleasant anticipation of acquaintance to be made.

There is in all this discourse a great deal of the first person singular. Indeed, it is impossible and wrong that there should not be. For if reading is not personal, if it is mere straw-fed imbibing and swallowing, it is nothing. And though I may quote Sir Thomas Browne, so delicately verbose, or Virginia Woolf or Horace or Kenneth Grahame, I can only cite their personal remarks in defence of my own. It is because Milton, writing on Education and consequently on Reading, failed to be personal, that his treatise is involved and vapid.

Reading must be so personal that the reader thinks of every character in relation to himself, every dogmatic remark as made to him only, and, as far as possible, applying only to him or his world. So may he stroll and dawdle in any century and any company, always in new territory, yet with familiar country all round him, 'full of noises, sounds and sweet airs, that give delight and hurt not.' If he is to be a good reader, he must be like the little horn-owl of which the chronicler tells, which was so taken with the sight of men dancing that it too jigged happily up and down on its perch, so engrossed that the fowlers caught it easily. That is he must live in his reading, so that when escape is necessary, it will be possible.

Then there will be no need, *'Quand vous serez bien vieille, au soir, à la chandelle,' to regret precious moments, and recall 'Ronsard me celebrait, du temps que j'étais belle.' Since in literature all precious moments are permanent.

* When you are quite old, in the evening, by candlelight
    Sitting close up to the fire, hemming and stitching
    Say, singing my verses and marvelling
    Ronsard sang songs of me, in the time when I was beautiful.

From 'Hélène' by Ronsard, a medieval trouvère.

[The translation is presumably by KD.]

For E.B.
Direz, chantant mes vers, en vous esmerveillant:
Ronsard me celebroit du temps que j'estois belle.

Thank you for a present you have given;
Sweet eyes and mouth, deigned me on certain days
Which out of dull years and the dull seven
I will recollect, my treasure a hundred ways.

This be my duty or pity; I give you my blessing,
Paid thanks, such prayers as I make, or what you would.
The charm outworn, there is no shame confessing,
Or standing glad for minutes that were good.

No drug or prayer will get this gift again,
This hour filled with gold others as we
Have found a torch, too hot with lovely pain;
Only to taste is this defended tree.

No use repainting, the dainty days are gone;
Only dreams gilt them with that simple light.
In this less happiness let us muddle on,
Not to forget until the black night.

[OUTLOOK, July 1938, signed with pseudonym 'Flip'. E.B. is probably Liz Brodie.]

On Getting to know a poet
(School exercise book; 'English Essay/1938')

To get to know a poet is to find out what are his objects and ideals, the message his songs sing and the effect he would attain. Before knowing a poet it is essential to penetrate beyond the first melody or cacophony of his words, spoken into the air, or suggesting sounds to the brain through the eye, and to see if there is a nut inside the delicate or ugly shell. Broadly speaking, the less nut, the sooner is the poet known. To be shallow and euphonious is the best method of catching the ear of multitudes, and naturally the poets with most to say are least attended and understood. A line of Rupert Brooke, 'Breathless we flung us on the windy hill,' or 'We will go down rose-crowned into the darkness' immediately sings to anyone young, sweetly enough, and its little meaning is soon clear. After you have read all Rupert's poetry, even his inconsequent letters, he has given you no more jewels. And poets like Brooke give a false value to the whole of poetry.

Fresh from his adolescent and simple ideals, suppose some casual sipping reader to find Dowson's villanelles or a sensual line or two of de Musset. The effect upon him is at first touch the same, and he may imagine himself to know these two more intense poets, and to know them the same sort as Rupert Brooke. He will continue in ignorance that these two, through their greater experience of unpleasentness, perhaps, had problems to face, and made use of poetry as a safety-valve as much as a means of telling the world and making money.

And even if a man may look on words, and if he pleaseth, through them pass, he must know what he is looking for beyond, and not think that the value of all poetry is gauged by a common criterion of his own manufacture. In order to appreciate poetry he must get to know the poet by being sure why he wrote. He must understand, say, the absurdities of Wordsworth, and not be put off the scent by Coleridge's exclamation marks. Diction must never by novelty of character fool a reader into admiration, or distract him from a possible meaning behind odd words and phrases.

This perfect reader must have a nose for clichés, yet see the poet he knows behind trite words. He must be prepared for devotion to melody and rhythm in a poet like Hopkins, and look for little else, nor balk at a certain baldness in some of Hardy's fierily sincere atheistic poems. Getting to know a poet involves a long journey through most of his available work, and through the knowledge of his way of life, his friends, his death, to the back of his mind.

Above all, anyone wishing to get to know any poet must avoid all but a very few anthologies, or he will find himself making estimates of Rupert from 'The Soldier', Siegfried Sassoon from 'Everyone suddenly burst out singing', or, worst of all, Sir William Watson from 'April'. There are of course anthologies which take their real job seriously, and try to help readers to get to know poets in a shorter time than by reading the whole of all their work. These books have to be compiled by men who have already got to know all the poets they present, and who now present the right impression in a few poems, because they know the impression to give.

It is often easier to get to know a poet without actually meeting him. So many poets, like so many other artists, are shy about what is most important to them and adopt an insincere joking or apologetic attitude about their poetry, quite misleadingly. Many of them can no more read their poems effectively than most composers can admirably sing their own music. I remember being particular [sic] disappointed when Michael Roberts read his poetry in his ugly Australian voice. He made it sound cheap; now, a year afterwards, I still have a feeling that perhaps it is cheap, the work for which I had so great admiration. Nor am I sure that the sight of Auden's face has not distorted my view of his poetry.

The criticism which a poet makes of other poets is often a guide to the poet himself. It shows his standards and ideals better even than his poetry itself. The criticisms of other poets, however, with other axes to grind, though self-revealing, are not so helpful for getting to know the criticised poet.

In any case it takes a long time to get to know a poet properly, and years of argument and dogmatic statement about him may finally persuade you that neither you nor any reader in the world can ever properly get to know him, or any other poet.

Misunderstanding
(posthumously published: OUTLOOK, spring 1980)

Cedric Kennedy lived in a rather tumbledown little cottage among the fields; and wrote poetry.

He used to send his poems to the editor of a very modern magazine, but none of them had ever been accepted. Cedric still hoped that one day he would think out a poem which would baffle even this hardened man, who, he was sure, never printed poems unless he could not make head or tail of them.

But poetry was not the only art of which Cedric imagined himself a master; he painted quite clever little watercolours of farms and the groups of tall trees which were almost as frequent as hedges in the fields about his cottage. He used to walk in these fields in the summer evenings, imagining all kinds of silly and beautiful happenings. The old hodmadod who stood rakishly in a field behind the cottage had even inspired a poem which began

cranes swing heaven on a girder
and the parasite
curling in the blue at the
end of it

The hodmadod did not come in until about twenty lines later, when he was hardly recognisable as

the leaning blackness mumbling
his tatters

Cedric liked best the little stream at the end of the cultivated part of his garden. Just the place, he used to think, for the Lord Fish to sit dangling his bait; and when he looked up to the bony downs with the evening light throwing long shadows in the dips and folds of them, he would say 'Thank God I'm a poet', and feel no end of a fellow.

But at other times, perhaps when he had had a little too much of his excellent cider (which was strong and bitter with pieces of cask floating about in it), or when he had had a very uncomplimentary letter from his editor, he used to think that perhaps he was missing something. He dreamed at these times of some beautiful girl, not very definitely imagined, with whom he would wander about this beautiful countryside, and whose company would complete the pleasure that the woods and fields gave him. Not a pretty girl, for Cedric considered prettiness not so much as a virtue, but rather as a social sin. Beauty he felt was quite different. But, as I said, he never defined this dream.

It was in one of his discontented moods that he set out one September morning to sketch, hoping that a long tramp over the fields would dispel his discontent. He had no more than a vague idea of his route, but he had plenty of lunch and a good pair of shoes, so that it mattered very little where he went. He walked hopefully out in a new direction. His road curled hedgily up to the downs, which looked particularly inviting that morning. Soon he had sketched a very old inn from the outside, and another, even older, from the inside. After he had come out into the sunlight again and wiped his mouth, he set off up a long hill, at the bottom of which the old inn stood. He walked slowly up this hill and more quickly down the other side; after that he went by a curling flat road for nearly half an hour. Then he stopped to mop his forehead and look about him for something to sketch. He noticed a high wall on his right stretching round the bend in front of him, and also round the bend behind him.

Now he came to think of it, he and the wall had been marching alongside each other for some miles. And behind such a wall there must be some vast estate, abounding in just the sort of things he wanted to sketch. The wall was not one of those with broken bottles along the top, so Cedric managed to climb over it, paints and all, in a very few minutes.

He came down into a wood, from which he emerged, covered with cobwebs and loose underbrush, into a wide field bounded by woods. He took out a piece of paper and began to sketch in the main composition of his picture.

When he had been there almost long enough for the rabbits to get used to him, and he was just touching in his first picture with small streaks of black, he saw a girl coming across the field towards him. She was small, with freckles and red-gold hair, and just the kind of nose which goes with freckles and red-gold hair.

She had a green dress on, simple, but (thought Cedric) probably expensive.

Cedric stood up. 'Good afternoon,' she said gravely, when she had come up to him, 'you ought to have asked first, you know. This is supposed to be private'. 'I'm sorry,' said Cedric, 'I just wondered what was over the wall, so I came over to see.' She smiled suddenly, wrinkling up her eyes and widening her small mouth. 'I don't really mind,' she said, 'let me look.'

Cedric told her about composition. In ten minutes he realised that his dream had come true. This was the girl of his imagination.

He looked at her interestedly to see what little points he had not thought of. Suppose he were to say 'I love you' without wasting any more time? She thought, 'I like his voice . . . I wonder . . . I shouldn't mind if he were to kiss me.' But she said, 'Got a match?' and Cedric after a confused 'Yes' found he had not.

'There's a squirrel,' she said, and they went over to the wood to explore, forgetting the paints. The wood was cool and exciting.

They played like children, chasing in and out of the shadows. Cedric took her by the shoulders and sat her down on a stump.

'This is the country of the leprechauns,' he said, 'We are enchanted.' And he told her how the Little People used to kidnap children by joining in their games of leapfrog, leading them always towards a hollow tree; and then, of course, just when they were least expecting it, they were inside the tree, with the little man over whom they had just leapt smiling down at them, and the other little men sitting round them, making shoes. 'You're good, aren't you?' said the girl, 'at telling stories, I mean . . . I would listen for hours.' 'Now,' thought Cedric, 'I must speak . . . tell her about my dream. I will just say, 'Would you mind another story?' and tell her. Then he would kiss her. That would be the place, just by her mouth, where a strand of hair hung loose. He looked at her, very longingly as he hoped. But she thought, 'Poor dear, he's bored, longing to get back to his paints. I'm too selfish and silly. Nothing ever comes right.' And she looked at Cedric rather sadly, just as he began to speak. 'Do you think . . . er . . . I mean, that is, would you mind . . .', he said and stopped a moment to collect his thoughts. The girl looked sadder than ever. 'Dreams,' she thought, 'never come true. Blast!' She forced a smile and completed his sentence for him '. . . if we go back to your paints? Of course not . . . I'm sorry. It's terrible of me to have kept you so long.' She spoke rather coldly in her disappointment, and Cedric thought, 'There . . . I knew it. I've made an ass of myself and been snubbed.'

They walked back in silence, save when Cedric tripped over a tree-stump, said 'Damn!' and blushed furiously. He packed up his paints, looking round at the woods, thinking what good times they might have had there, and said awkwardly, 'Thanks, er, well . . . Goodbye, and well, thanks.' 'Goodbye,' said the girl still more coldly. 'Come here whenever you like.' 'Thanks,' said Cedric again, feeling very foolish and incomplete.

Of course he never did go there again. He lives in Chelsea with a beard and six mistresses, indulging in vodka and red cigarettes, and painting on occasion post-paulo Georgian pictures (putting the paint on in the latest way, by stepping in a bath of it and walking on the canvas).

The girl in green is a large red woman, who rides to hounds five days in the week. She has forgotten that she ever had a green dress, but she still prides herself on an ability to read faces.

And if Cedric had only grown his beard sooner, his face would never have betrayed him so tragically, and this story would have been unwritten. Perhaps.

[Given the magazine by Lionel Tidmarsh, one of his old English masters. The quotations are from Douglas's own poems.]

New Year
(OUTLOOK, April 1938)

I have never met a man who kept his New Year promises: seldom are any seriously made. For, after all, the essence of such resolutions is no more than acknowledgement of the obvious symbolism of fresh year and new leaf. And but for a difficulty in remembering the new fourth figure, when I date my letters (which is not often), I hardly notice New Year, and never sit up to see it in. And for those of my generation who do, there can be little meaning in the ceremony, as yet.

But now I have undertaken to write of it, I cannot ignore the significance time will give it, for me as for all men upon the earth. I have noticed how old people find their own importance in each death of the year. No dream of recreation or progress is in their minds, but the thought only of the days, more lovely still in the

distance, when they were intolerant and young, unable to see the
end of all their hopes. Now in the twisted sinews, the witty
remarks superannuated, the travesty each looking-glass presents
them with, they see each year more plainly the other side of life,
the pattern reversed which seemed so fine to them. They know
this is no country for old men, this new world where they are the
shelved and tolerated; and each New Year is symbolised for them
by 'Auld Lang Syne.'

Perhaps I avoid New Year in my thoughts because I am afraid
of it; because, like Margaret grieving over Golden-grove unleav-
ing, I am already unconsciously shivering at the picture of death.
For now I do think of it I am filled with fear; that same fear which
is inspired, inexplicably, by perfectly blue skies and the poem
about the Last Buccaneer and the pleasant isle of Avés; fear that

When I've spun
My last thread, I shall perish on the shore,

with nothing done of the things which I have wanted.

The first of January, a day like other days in a cold season, has
put on these associations like a mask of Beelzebub, and now
comes dressed in clothes which are not her own. For there are
many other days when the New Year might more fittingly arrive.
All changes of season; from green to gold, gold to leaflessness,
and nudity to green again, might mark a year's ending and
beginning, particularly the change from winter to spring. Or
Christ's day from which the centuries are dated, might mark each
year's birthday, too, and Christmas begin the year in a pleasant
atmosphere of goodwill. But the interest taken in New Year now
would not be strong enough to achieve the revolution.

It was not always of such little significance though, as the
whisky and pipers of Hogmanay prove. Probably New Year was
an important time in Celtic Britain, when Druids performed
strange ceremonies by torchlight among their squat stones, and
the old year ended for many unfortunates with a ritual knife-
stroke. Maybe on this night the ancient devils were abroad, and
could be called to service by an adequate combination of charms
and circles.

Perhaps even now in other countries some beating of old
drums and traditional dancing makes up for England's apathy to
New Year. I cannot remember any particular ceremonies: save
that in the North Italian town of Gorizia it is celebrated by a
torchlight procession of prelates and choristers round the town,

interminably chanting 'Ave Maria,' while the townsfolk doff their
hats. There are indeed great traditional possibilities in New Year:
it is a time when many outlandish rites might be practised.
Mediaeval New Years were made important by the great fairs of
France and Germany.

But none of these possibilities has been exploited. The New
Year is no longer, whatever we may say of it, a season of any great
significance to the majority of people. Perhaps the wireless will
restore its old character, with a text of

> Ring out, wild bells, to the wild sky.

This is the only poem which springs to mind at the mention of
New Year, and it is a terrible poem to those old people, for whom
each New Year is awful and significant, who hear with realisation
and sadness the wild, inexorable bells.

Going Away
(OUTLOOK, April 1938)

The man was large and pompous: he ought to have been called
Mr Troutbeck, or Purdle; no doubt he was. And as he said
good-bye to his wife in the next compartment, I saw that his nose
was very large. Large noses always tempt me, and as the train
began to move, I said: 'Excuse me, sir,' and pulled this one. The
train gathered speed, and he and the platform were hidden by a
bend.

But how different it would have been if the train had stopped
again after a few yards, as trains do, with Mr Purdle free to storm
up the platform behind his injured nose. This absurd episode
would have been incomplete and disastrous, as many more
serious have been for the same reason. For a great measure of the
art of living lies in knowing when to remain and when to go
away. Many men are honoured as martyrs who should be pitied,
because they did not know when to go away, when to let 'I dare
not' wait upon 'I would,' like the poor, but prudent, cat in the
adage. Sir Walter Raleigh survived Queen Elizabeth's reign by a
series of opportune departures. He knew how long the Queen's
mind would be taken up with the results of one expedition, and
when it was likely to swing away at a more dangerous tangent.

Between shore and shore on a seven-day cruise a very touching and complete 'affaire' may be begun and finished: and, though hackneyed, 'I never saw him again' still retains its appeal at the end of a character description. It is not only on the stage that an effective exit is desirable.

Moreover, as going away is part of the art of living, so it is in itself an art; and to acquire it you must know how to deal with many situations and people: be able to see, as it were, both sides of the corner, or to forget one if you will: to realise the unimportance of some departures, and not to make overmuch of others because they are of a kind traditionally regarded as important.

It is very often only in early childhood that we attach the correct relative importance to our goings and comings. It sometimes happens then that we realise when someone is going away for good, without being told of it, and that while one leave-taking is not important, another will change our small world. But this is a very short period sandwiched between the first days, when life is like a tape-measure slowly unrolling, whose measurements are not yet visible, and the older years when everything is shaken into and out of proportion many times, and may never settle down.

After assessing the importance of the art of going away, let us touch upon its uses. Going away is of course primarily symbolic, not only of an ending but a fresh beginning. Many years ago the film producers discovered this, and even now it is not uncommon to see the hero and heroine disappearing at the end of a film into a distance where their dreams will presumably come true.

Going away conjures up so many memories, good and bad, of exultant escape or regretful leaving, for so many people, that there is no end to the good and bad things which may be said of it. But I have often thought that there would be something very attractive about a perpetually flitting life. If a man had enough money, he might make a profession of going away, and it is conceivable that he might never be bored for the rest of his life.

For the world, as we are always hearing from unwelcome acquaintances, is a small place, and after going round it a few times, there would be no regret at leaving some friends behind, for the anticipation of meeting others and the knowledge that none were left behind for long would outweigh regret. For in this flitting life unlimited indulgence is for once better than moderation. The only profession which rivals going away is that of settling down. But death, which must be a jolt to the settled man, only takes the traveller off on a fresh and interesting journey, since to him all new country is familiar.

❥

Douglas sat for an open scholarship at Oxford in December 1937. On his examination paper for the General Essay he left jottings towards his essay.

❥

Words

Words are a trumpet, a difficult instrument: are bricks to build with, flowers to make a pattern. Intricate or simple, they are treasure to play with, like diamonds stones to the beast, and useless, but to the connoiseur most valuable in the world. Since the beginning of Time man has amused himself with words, and from his own life added more to the treasure. Like some enchanted gold it grows greater with use.

❥

The images from the examination room were to reappear in a poem of 1943, 'Behaviour of Fish in an Egyptian Tea Garden': 'she sits alone at the table, a white stone/useless except to a collector, a rich man.'

Douglas gained an Open Exhibition for entry into Merton College in October 1938. He had sat the examinations in History, there being no English Sixth in his school at that time, but his place was granted on the understanding that he would read English. Edmund Blunden, who cherished his own time at Christ's Hospital before the First World War and kept a keen eye on its talented pupils, regarding himself very much as an 'Old Blue' author, was to be Douglas's tutor.

❥

28 January 1938   *Christ's Hospital, Sussex*

Dear Mr Blunden, Thank you very much for your letter. I have shewn it to Mr Roberts, who asked me to write to you originally, and to Mr Macklin, who has taken over most of my English work from Mr Roberts, now that I have dropped History. Mr Roberts

agreed with you more or less entirely, I believe, but he will write
to you himself.

Mr Macklin however, since most of the Old Blue authors are by
no means fresh ground to me (and he thinks I should tackle
something on which my mind is more or less a blank) suggests
that I should study the one least known to me and least noticed by
the school English curriculum, Leigh Hunt. He had already
started me off (before your letter arrived), upon a course of
drama, to specialise in the Elizabethans, but including some work
on mimes and miracle plays from classical times.

I have an Oxford Edition of Chaucer's Works which I read for
my own amusement but I am afraid I have not read any comment
on them, except G. K. Chesterton's book.

If this compromise between your plan and Mr Macklin's
original one of general reading and Elizabethan poetry and
drama will do I will start on it as soon as possible. I have already
begun the drama, which is keeping me very busy. I hope this
does not seem to you an impatient and impertinent rejection of
your advice: if you still think it would be better for me to take all
the O.B. authors I can start work on them as soon as your letter
arrives to say so.

Yours sincerely, *Keith Douglas*

13 May 1938   *Christ's Hospital, Sussex*

Dear Mr Blunden, I am writing to tell you how I have been
spending my time during last term and the Easter holidays. I
don't know whether Mr Macklin, or Mr Roberts has written to
you, but in any case you may be interested to have my own
account of it.

I began by reading some miracle plays and various early
comedies, Ralph Roister Doyster and Gammer Gurton among
them. Simultaneously with these I studied Leigh Hunt's life and
works and wrote an essay on him and another on his poetry. I
also read Allardyce Nicholl on Masks, Mimes and Miracles, and
on The Development of the theatre. I took notes on this but did
not write anything actually about it, although I used it with
reference to other essays.

I read two plays each of Lyly, Peele, and Greene, and wrote on
all three of them together. Then I read Nashe's Lenten Stuff and
reread Tamburlaine taking notes on the verse. After that I wrote a

very hasty essay on the Verse of Tamburlaine, the matter of which pleased Messrs Macklin and Roberts more than any of my other efforts, although the expression, being hurried, was bad.

In the holidays I read a long essay on Lyly by Bond, and all his plays, and wrote notes on them, from which I am now writing an essay. I managed to read Heywood's Woman Killed with Kindness — and Sense and Sensibility and Amaryllis at the Fair as a change.

Another book I read was James Hilton's And Now Goodbye. I wonder what you think of his writing? I have only read four of his books, and taking them as short stories — which, except for Lost Horizon, they seemed to be — I admire them.

I have been attempting some short stories myself, and have sent two in for a Short Story Competition run by the Cambridge Literary Agency.

This term I shall go on working at Elizabethan drama, which really interests me.

I hope this letter will not bother you, and that you wanted to know what I have told you.

Yours sincerely, *Keith Douglas*

P.S. I am sending 2 pictures to the Sussex Art Exhibition if I can finish them in time.

16 May 1938   *12 Woodstock Close, Oxford*

My dear Douglas, It looks as though you have been digging in with excellent energy. I shall not know how to employ you when you come up! but the philological side will keep you busy as you are aware. And you may have made time for the Fine Arts lectures here (Michael Holroyd) which are understood to be first class. I am very curious to see your paintings. Some years since we had M. Easton at Merton, who combined the English School with all sorts of artistic activity, even a beard, which was not too formal.

If you should one day publish a new edn. of C. Lamb's Dramatic Specimens I will buy several copies!

Please don't imitate my Punctuation and scrawl, I get more primeval every day under the influence of Walter de Merton's deathmask. There's some chance of my visiting C.H. this term and I shall see you then I hope.

Yours sincerely, *E. Blunden*

13 September 1938 *The Rectory, Withyham*

Dear Mr Blunden, This is a letterful of questions, which I hope will not bother you too much.

1   I have received a notice requiring me to come into residence on October 7th. Is this an earlier date than the day on which the whole College comes up? I have heard that freshmen are required to come up earlier, and was not certain whether October 7th was the earlier date or not.

2   Would it be unusual for me to have luggage, etc., sent to Merton 2 or 3 days before I am required to come into residence?

3   I have not been able to get a list of College rules — to whom should I apply for these?

4   Some months ago I had sent me from Merton College a statement that the amount of my Exhibition was £30 p.a., and that a further grant was to be made, of £50, subject to adjustment if 'further emolument' was obtained. Well, further emolument has been obtained, but I still need the £50 p.a. Would it be possible for you to find out what adjustment,

5   if any, has taken place; and can you tell me how this money would be paid, or allowed me?

I am sorry to buzz at you with so many queries, some of which must seem to you pointless — but I shall be bewildered enough even when all these are answered. When I see you I shall still be loaded with a charge of more particular enquiries.

My address will be the one at the top of this letter until the 19th, from which date until the 27th September I shall be at Stakers, Southwater, Horsham. After the 27th until I go up to Merton I shall be at St Hugh's Cottage, Oakleigh Rd., Little Common, Bexhill. Not the least of my difficulties is this continual migration while I am making arrangements.

Yours sincerely, *Keith Douglas*

Douglas arrived at Merton on 7 October 1938 and moved into room 2,2 in Fellows Quad. He took little part in the literary life of the university but at Blunden's suggestion did meet the poet Margaret Stanley Wrench, then in her fourth year at Somerville, and a friendship centred on horses rather than on poetry, grew between them. Occasionally he met John Waller, who took his poems

---

for *Bolero* and later for *Kingdom Come*, and J. C. Hall, who took poems for *Fords and Bridges*.

❧

16 February 1939   12 Woodstock Close, Oxford

Dear Douglas, We should be very happy if your Mother and you could have supper here (a very informal matter) on Saturday evening. 7.30 or so — and you know the No. 4 to Woodstock Close.

Yours sincerely, *Very Old Blue*

17 February,

This was ready for delivery but now I have yr. note, so with regret I leave the matter for the present: our Sunday is a difficult day, but I shall *try* to call at your room about four. Make no difference in your plans on that account. *E.B.*

26 March 1939   Preston Cottage, Bexhill

Dear Mr Blunden, I don't know whether this will catch you in time, but I hoped to see you at the end of term, and this letter will have to say what I meant to say then. The week of no exams during P. Mods was more taken up than I expected, because I had to do some of Hamo's share of preparing for Anglo Saxon, since he was busy about his other subjects. Most of the time here since I came down has been taken up doctoring a sick horse with a constantly renewed rash which takes half the day to wash and the other half to anoint. My essay is only half done, and will therefore probably arrive written in pencil on a notebook during intervals of cycling in France.

Meanwhile I have not obtained two certificates from you which I meant to get at the end of term. One is for the Mitchell City of London people and they want it at the end of this month — this, if you can conscientiously sign it, is to be a tutor's certificate of residence and satisfactory progress.

It is rather important that I should have this one, because if I don't get the Mitchell money I shall be about £12 short at the beginning of the next term for paying my battels. The other is a certificate of residence to be sent up immediately at the beginning of next term, and as they are very late with the money as a rule, I should like to send it the moment I arrive. The Mitchell one is to say I have been in residence, the other to say I am in residence. If you could send me the Mitchell certificate, to this address as soon as you have time, I should be very glad.

All that remains to do to my essay is to write it. That is to say I have got all the notes and the general outline, and references and quotations, so I will send it as soon as possible.

Yours sincerely, *Keith Douglas*

P.S. If the certificate comes to this address I will see it is sent to the Mitchell people at once, even if I am in France. I have brought home Chaucer, Gower, Saintsbury. *KCD*

27 March 1939   *12 Woodstock Close, Oxford*

Dear Douglas, I send the tutor's certificate for the Mitchell trustees; the other you shall have when you come up. And I have sent one to Lewes, for the County authority.

I am sure you will have agreeable adventures in France, where I shall go for 3 or 4 days before next term.

Think well over your whole course ahead while you are seated on some Normandy hill in the sun. You have now had 2 terms and time runs away. Consider exactly what the Statutory scheme of the English school is, and apply your powers to it as to any other problem. Map out a way of progressive reading, such as will cover the great authors and particular works which the examiners require, and allow too for any special tastes of your own. But the chief thing to aim at is a continuous view of English literary achievement, with its 'beautiful variety,' in which there is still method and unity. You can only just cram the necessary reading in, before the Schools will be upon you.

Yours ever, *E. Blunden*

[14 June 1939]   *Fellows 2.2.*

Dear Mr Blunden, Please may I have your recommendation of the renewal of a grant of £50 from the Mitchell City of London Charity and Educational Foundation? I am a little late applying so I have dated my letter of application from tomorrow (15th), Thursday,

and hope I may have your chit by then. The essay notes are
going well, but getting complicated.

Yours sincerely, *Keith Douglas*

On 3 September 1939 war was declared. Douglas, who had
planned to spend the winter semester in Munich, enlisted at
once.

[*11 September 1939*]   *The Rectory, Withyham*

Dear Mr Blunden, I shan't be coming up next term being a
Calvary Trooper at the moment and getting a commission in about
6/7 months. If I am about when the war ends — or 'above
ground', as the O.T.C. Colonel puts it so neatly and unoriginally
— I hope I'll be back. If you'd like to set me some long-distance
essays 'Shakespeare's Historical Plays and their bearing on C.T.
Vol III', or 'The Language of Chaucer's Knight as compared with
that of an English Cavalry Officer' (which has been done by
Bairnsfather anyway), please set them and I'll try to get one or
two done. I wonder what is happening to you? I hope you'll stay on
at Merton. I saw C. T. Hatten late of C.H. who is to be a Gunner
Officer, (also Lawrance, who preceded him as Senior Grecian).
Hamo had not been called up when I last heard of him, but he will
be, perhaps into the same lot as I go to. [Hamo Sassoon, Siegfried's nephew and a close friend of Douglas at Merton.]

Thank heavens I can't see what is going to happen to us all as
clearly as you must be able to. Perhaps there'll be a German
Revolution before I get through my training.

I have managed to read a lot of Saintsbury Literary History,
some Dekker, Utopia, T. Tusser, Defense of Poesie, John
Heywood, and other early drama filling in where I got to at
Housey. Malory has also taken up my time. Just lately I have been
too occupied for anything in the way of reading, but now I know
what's being done with me I have nothing to occupy me until I'm
called up.

Tomorrow I'm hiring a car for the tremendous sum of £3.5s to
collect stuff from Merton. I'm not allowed to pay 17/6 and drive it
myself because I'm under 21. At 19 however I'm quite old enough

to be allowed to be used in keeping the country safe for other road-users.

I hoped to see you while I was up being enlisted, but didn't have time to go out to Woodstock and you apparently didn't come to college while I was there as your letters in the lodge remained untouched and continued to accumulate during my three days up.

Yours sincerely, *Keith Douglas*

P.S. I never got to München.

19 September 1939   *Merton College*

My dear Douglas, I deplore this vast disturbance which has broken in on your university career, I can only hope that you'll get some compensations in the cavalry (or petrolry) and soon return to us full of energy and literary impulse. My view of the future is a bit wonky, but I rather imagine that as events have been so surprising in recent years the present matter too will not proceed 'as planned', and more extraordinary turns of history lie ahead for us. Keep reading what you can. You will hit on things that take a deep meaning, and impress very powerfully, under this whirling sky. I like the list you sent me, including those honest plain wise men Dekker and Tusser. Hamo's movements are as yet unknown to me. Ask C.H. to allow you something for the unusual expense forced on you of moving from Merton. I dare say they will wish to help a young Cavalier. My own case is that I stay here for at least this term: some people in and out of Merton will want tuition. I don't know how things will turn out later, the old hacks may have to take the road again; I wish people would have thought more deeply about peace and war. Sorry about München. But perhaps the day will come.

Please remember me kindly to your mother —
Yours ever, *E.B.*

In October, his call-up postponed for a term at least, Douglas returned to Oxford for what proved to be a whole year. In the Michaelmas term he assisted in a production of Dryden's *Secular Masque*, with Blunden playing Chronos. In

May 1940 he co-edited with Alec Hardie *Augury: An Oxford Miscellany*. Their introduction follows.

Introduction to *Augury*

It has become the custom for the first pages of any book, particularly of anthologies, to be devoted to titles, acknowledgements, and an introduction, guardedly written by the Editor — an anticipation of criticism. This custom further prescribes that this introduction should act as an overture, inserted to create the required atmosphere, but to be glossed over while hastening on to the main contents. Sometimes there are exceptions to this code; the Introduction is presumed to be a précis of the policy, purpose and contents. The Editor's refraining from expressing himself adequately can often provide a general hypothesis for censure. The quality of the pie is judged by the thickness of the pastry.

Our policy is the occasion; it has no carefully defined boundaries, no exclusive tenets which have to be observed. If any conclusions or trends are to be found, then Oxford has provided them. It is possible that some masterpiece has been rejected through lack of appreciation and competence on the part of the Editors, who have endeavoured to combine a respect for literature with a certain local consideration.

It was hoped that Oxford could offer work that was worthy of recording at this time, as even now it must claim to be one of the few remaining institutions in which liberty of thought and speech is actively encouraged. A great metamorphosis came upon the city in October 1939. Colleges were thinly populated; many rooms were stripped bare; sand-bags were clumsily guarding precious walls. The quiet atmosphere had been disturbed by the briskness of business departments; it was obvious that the sentimental Oxford had to contend with a determined foe. At that time the present work was projected in the hope that it would show not ony some degree of merit and thought still existing in Oxford, but also some way through the seeming morass of public ideas. The result has been an odd assemblage, and so representative, for in this miscellany fact jolts against hopes, tradition against novelty.

The nature of the poetry in this volume is not nearly so

introspective or gloomy as might have been feared. Some is cheerful and some admittedly cynical. But most of these poets survey the world still as placidly as one should who looks out from such an ancient standpoint as this university. The emotions expressed are as a rule about more ordinary and permanent things than the situation this year, and, though not introspective, most of the poetry is pleasantly personal. If it leaves no great thoughts or thunderous lines in your mind, at least it may in mass reflect a kind solidity and some comfort. It is reassuring to find that love and nature are still inspiration for good poetry, and we were glad that most of the stark and bitter writing was so bad that it could not be included. The poets in this anthology are not with the times, but in most of their thought hark back or forward to a better age. In an amorphous world it is an encouragement to see form returning to poetry, and trust again in what men used to think were essentially great and good things.

A friendly critic, who has been induced to look through the volume, remarks that these writings confirm his general observation on the younger people of England at present: 'I greatly admire' he says, 'this stoicism, but it is something handsomer than that: I honour this refusal equally of hopes and despairs, this willingness to watch life and occasion, this acceptance of the chances which may either bless or ravage any one man or woman. The style, as well as the substance, of the rising race of poets seems to me to promise a world worth living in, if some temporary disadvantages are removed.'

Youth is a poetical thing; it prefers to pour out a full soul in some verse form; emotional tension seems to be slackened when in Prose. It is a paradoxical modesty which allows the use of the medium and matter of Shakespeare and Milton, but which hesitates before the greatness of Macaulay and Coleridge. Consequently most of the Prose has been written by senior and already well-known members. The matter is usually informative, but the authors' maturity has made it provocative. It is a miscellaneous collection; the subject-matter was the choice of the author. Not only do we delight that so many senior members have contributed, but we are honoured that their contributions are on their own special theme; so the authority supporting them has considerably raised the worth of the articles. If any conclusion may be drawn from this Prose, it is that culture in its widest sense is still of interest in Oxford. Oxford is doing more, it is endeavouring to keep an active interest in the Arts by not allowing theory to overwhelm practice.

Our thanks and gratitude for help in this volume must reach many. First, to Edmund Blunden we are deeply appreciative for being the *fons et origo* of this project. Throughout his energy and ready advice have been an impetus to us.

We owe much to Basil Blackwell for the co-operation and enthusiasm that he has often displayed. We are deeply sensible of his affection for Oxford. In acting as 'agents' Daphne Aye Moung and Roger Lancelyn Green proved indefatigable.

But our largest measure of thanks we must give to all contributors who have so generously presented their work to be treated in as arbitrary a fashion as we wished.

On the Nature of Poetry
(AUGURY, 1940)

Poetry is like a man, whom thinking you know all his movements and appearance you will presently come upon in such a posture that for a moment you can hardly believe it a position of the limbs you know. So thinking you have set bounds to the nature of poetry, you shall as soon discover something outside your bounds which they should evidently contain.

The expression 'bad poetry' is meaningless: critics still use it, forgetting that bad poetry is not poetry at all.

Nor can prose and poetry be compared any more than pictures and pencils: the one is instrument and the other art. Poetry may be written in prose or verse, or spoken extempore.

For it is anything expressed in words, which appeals to the emotions either in presenting an image or picture to move them; or by the music of words affecting them through the senses; or in stating some truth whose eternal quality exacts the same reverence as eternity itself.

In its nature poetry is sincere and simple.

Writing which is poetry must say what the writer has himself to say, not what he has observed others to say with effect, nor what he thinks will impress his hearers because it impressed him hearing it. Nor must he waste any more words over it than a mathematician: every word must work for its keep, in prose, blank verse, or rhyme.

And poetry is to be judged not by what the poet has tried to say; only by what he has said.

🜲

Douglas's poems had been appearing in *The Cherwell* since the second term of his second year. In the third term, he became its editor; on occasion being so short of usable material that he filled the space with his own work, disguising it under pseudonyms such as 'Peter Hatred' and 'John Oligarch'. As editor of the only undergraduate weekly to have survived the war, he took on the role of spokesman.

🜲

Jeunesse Oblige
(THE CHERWELL, 27 April 1940)

Here the follies of youth and the idiocies of old age flourish as nowhere else: and winter, which damps youthful activities without much impairing the indoor life of old age, has departed. It is summer terms that we are going to have in mind when we ourselves become the denizens of winter. And meanwhile we are pledged to youth this term as a matter of duty, while the rest of the world, undeterred by spring and summer, grows older and older. It has taken but a short time for the superstition to take hold again, that we are fighting a race of submen, of whom every member from birth is certainly a brutal moron. But even this will not long be enough to provide the family with destructive breakfast topics, and the words pacifist and coward will soon be as synonymous as they were a quarter of a century ago. In no time at all it will be once more *de rigeur* to put nearly everyone against a wall: and the Englishman with his traditional modesty will consider himself the salt of the earth and the saviour of it. Not the Englishman who fights, but he who stays at home and doesn't know what we at Oxford are coming to. And as long as he and his kind condemn us and rant at the enemy and the pacifist in terms of the last generation but one, we may be satisfied that to be young is still as always the most useful and heroic occupation. It is still the part of youth, as far as possible to stem the foolishness of a dying generation and in time to redress it. Why youth is so soon forgotten is more than we can say. Perhaps we shall know when we ourselves have forgotten it.

This term we hope to produce a consistently improving CHERWELL, in the intransitive sense. But there must be more material from which to construct it. You are still urged to give evidence that more undergraduates can produce something worth the notice of the rest of the university. Linocuts, woodcuts, wood engravings, and any other form of illustration which can be printed from the illustrator's own block, will be welcomed; and we are anxious to print them, though a fairly high standard will be set. Owing to the cost of paper and the lack of wartime advertisers, the CHERWELL cannot afford to print posters: but it will be on the bookstalls each week, and if you have any interest at all in the last undergraduate journal of Oxford or Cambridge, you will at least go and see what is in it. We have tried to assemble a staff this term which drinks less sherry and does more work, and hope their efforts may content you. There will not be any regular competitions this term, but prizes will be given for any outstanding writing or illustration submitted.

We commend to your notice the immediate appearance of the Oxford Miscellany of Prose and Verse for which contributions were solicited during the last two terms. It is published by Basil Blackwell under the title *Augury*, and for the price of four shillings and sixpence. It contains three new poems by Edmund Blunden, and a fourth which has appeared in THE CHERWELL: an article on amateur drama in Oxford by Neville Coghill: and two poems by C. S. Lewis. Among past and present members of the university who contribute prose or poetry are John Waller, Geoffrey Matthews, Norman Bradshaw, Margaret Stanley-Wrench, Paul Engle, J. C. Hall, Keith Douglas, and S. G. Watts. There is also an article by the publisher.

Comparatively few people in the University know of the existence of a private theatre at John Masefield's ex-house on Boars Hill. Performances of ballet by the pupils of Lydia Sokolova, and of music by members of the university, were given there last summer term; in which the majority of undergraduates showed a characteristic lack of interest. This term it might be used again, if there is any support for the idea. [. . .]

Editorial
(THE CHERWELL, 4 May 1940)

Hey, Persephone, have you forgotten? The first of May and what happens? You forget your cue, and instead of reporting your entry we have to put in a fable instead.

An artist was engaged, one pleasant summer afternoon, in portraying upon his canvas with facile hand, a herd of cows browsing in a watery meadow. Beginning with the cow on the left, and including both background and foreground he found in course of time that he had completed a masterpiece. His delight at this achievement vented itself in an uncommon benevolence, which centred for the time being on the right hand cow, the animal he had drawn last. Realising, with some strange feral intelligence, that the picture was finished, the right hand cow moved from her place in the landscape and advanced towards the artist, who welcomed her with endearments. But the animal first halted some twenty yards away, and coyly pretended to ignore him. The artist redoubled his enticements, and went so far as to pluck some grass, which he extended invitingly in the direction of the cow. At last she moved towards him again, but with the utmost diffidence: and it was only with the failing light of evening that the artist and the cow reached terms of close acquaintance. Coy though she had been before, the cow now became almost embarrasingly forward. She licked the artist affectionately with her rough tongue, and breathed upon him her verdant breath. He in his turn fascinated by the softness of her coat, stroked and restroked it, from the folds of her neck along her smooth flank. It was while he meditatively patted her beautiful hindquarters that the cow transferred his masterpiece to her insides, with a few easy strokes of her tongue.

The moral is that there is more than one way of beginning an editorial.

Two special numbers of THE CHERWELL, still conceived only as clouds hovering in the atmosphere, where they may be seen on fine days drifting above Cherville House, are deserving of a more concrete existence. They are the Sport number which might have appeared last term, and a Contempt For Our Elders number, for both of which contributions are urgently requested. From to-day you are asked to regard all older persons with hostile and critical suspicion for at least two hours a week, and to submit the results of your scrutiny in writing to this paper. At least one elder person will be allowed to have at you in the same number.

By a happy accident, one of THE CHERWELL staff was passing the locked door of Merton library at dead of night, when the medieval essence of Duns Scotus passed easily through its woodwork, and accosted him in friendly Latin. Although the spirit at first declined, he was at length persuaded to write an article for THE CHERWELL, which is now in the hands of translators. Since the transparent scholar was working on this script until after cockcrow on some mornings last week, he has been compensated with a free seat at the Scala this week. And if he comes in late you will not have to stand up and let him through.

THE CHERWELL proposes in the near future to publish a SKIPPING RHYME SUPPLEMENT. Those of you who skipped in early youth may remember that children accompany their efforts with various doggerel rhymes, some of which must be very ancient indeed. If enough of these can be collected, they should be at least as interesting as our usual poetry: and some more erudite person may write us an explanation of their origins.

The A.R.P. conscience is not yet dead. A torch fell overboard into the river last week, and could be seen shining on the riverbed. Its owner immediately divested himself of every garment and sped like a plummet to retrieve the telltale light. As the chief constable reminds us, it is particularly necessary that no electric lights should be dropped in the water; for they would be easily visible to any German airman equipped with polaroid spectacles. The rescuer paddled modestly off into the darkness and refused to divulge his identity.

The Editor would be glad to hear of anyone who is prepared to contribute a weekly article, report, or story, to THE CHERWELL. Anyone interested should send a specimen article, story, or report. Meanwhile being still without such contributions the editor must leave his editorial and contrive to fill some more blank pages further on.

The Yellow Book
(THE CHERWELL, 18 May 1940)

The butterfly searches always for the great sun, and as he passes erratically in the light of it, we see him as admirable, a poet on a splendid errand. On closer examination it appears that he has an absurd body, and a face no more splendid nor admirable than a spider's. At the end of a short life he has accomplished nothing, picking and sipping while worm and ant work beneath in the earth. He flutters too, symbolically, over the pages of the *Yellow Book*, that strange quarterly in which is shut up so much 'decadent' expression. The butterfly is the device and image of his portrayers. Like him, though far more self-consciously, the young intellectuals of the eighteen-nineties strove towards the sun: not towards the great light of the heavens but towards a brilliant and artificial luminary of their imagination. Their goal was so bright and minute that they often lost sight of it to become entangled in their own intricacies: contributors to the *Yellow Book* laboured to be different, more intense, more dazzling, more yellow.

This is still the aim of some young people, but they cannot develop it to so fine an art. To-day does not encourage the inspired self-consciousness and perversity, or such devotion to affected detail. The decadents who produced the *Yellow Book* became entangled in their own complications, as the eye is entangled by the involved patterns and lines of their drawings, or the ear bemused by the innumerable turns of their literary style. Their quest was splendid, but their methods were necessarily corrupt; and their book is the record of a vain search, doomed from the start, carried out with the consciousness of impending fate. The ambition of them all was to catch some splendid moment, to hold it in the hand, turn it over and over like a jewel. Their stories end not with a moral but with a moment. A moment is caught in their poetry, in their illustration, poising a dancer in the air, or recording a fleeting expression. They sought thus to gain the essential virtue of life, working in a feverish hurry against Time and Death.

In such haste as this, fighting an imminent death by consumption, Aubrey Beardsley, who may be called the greatest of them all, postured away his life. He might have been the embodied spirit of the *Yellow Book*. His art made ordinary things precious and sinister, imbued with all the unhealthiness and hectic quality of the movement itself. And unhealthiness, the last energy of a high fever, is the mark of all typically decadent art and writing. Those who could not bring themselves to be unhealthy, succeeded with hardly an exception, only in being sentimental.

But the *Yellow Book* is important because it contains not only the story of their failure, an the explanation of it; but that beauty which attends fever and unnatural animation. Only one writer may be said to be of the movement without death's hand appearing in his work: Max Beerbohm mastered the momentary beauties of incident and style, and a less bitter humour. Henry Harland might have this claimed for him too, but although he contributed to the *Yellow Book*, he was too lukewarm to be a member of the movement: he wore it a moment like a new cloak. The poetry in the *Yellow Book* forms a link with the (no less unhealthy) French romantic poets, in particular, Verlaine and Rimbaud: the Frenchmen and contributors to the *Yellow Book* exchanged translations and titles. Some of the *Yellow Book's* contributors have continued to work until quite recently. Kenneth Grahame and Edmund Sullivan are not long dead.

But for the most part they are gone. Those who were mediocrities because of their mediocrity: those who were great lights because inevitably they burnt themselves out. Upon them all the mark of the butterfly was too strong; a thoughtlessness and inconsequence more colloquially expressed in Tararaboomdeay, the most popular song of the period. The majority of readers have forgotten all their productions except perhaps those of Symons' scholarship, but the *Yellow Book* still glares on some shelves and in some second-hand bookshops to recall one of youth's most beautiful follies and achievements.

Drunk: a short story
(THE CHERWELL, 27 April 1940)

He was sitting among the crowd of officers at the pavement tables, the cavalrymen in sky-blue cloaks, some infantrymen wearing darker uniforms and all with their brilliant tinny swords flung magnificently in the path of passers-by. I noticed him from the other side of the street, bright among all that brightness: his head bowed over the wine-soiled table-cloth was covered with a black and yellow handkerchief, making a wasp's face at me. And when he looked up and beckoned to me, I crossed over, partly from curiosity and partly from thirst, to sit and drink with him. I was not surprised when he spoke to me in English; I am obviously English, I fear undisguisably. Perhaps he was English, too, for his voice had no accent when he said, without preamble, 'There is a story about this poem.'

He read the poem in a voice as harsh as the claret, before me in its green-glass globular bottle. The officers turned to this sound of rising speech, breaking in upon their liquor-hum; I remember the clink of their swords. He never lowered his voice, but read the last verse clearly in their faces:

All this the bottle says, that I have quite
Poured out. The wine slides in my throat and grieves.
Over and over the street is repeated with sunlight:
The flutes sound in the wineshop, out of sight.

I said: 'I have heard them,' and thought, now for the story.

'The man lived,' he said, 'at Peacehaven.' Imagination wrote the incongrous word across the blue back of the soldier in front of me. 'He lived only to write poetry, and to spend his mother's money on the wines with odd names. His largest ambition was to have a poem accepted by one of those exclusive little magazines which live chiefly on the subscriptions of their contributors. When he was twenty-two he wrote something he knew was really good: the long words and similes fell over one another delightfully, and when he had written it he thought of a meaning for it too.

'There was a sort of competition in one of these magazines, and to his mind there could be no doubt that this was the prize poem. He wanted to celebrate. He had a few bottles of Liebfraumilch in the house that time, so he drank the lot. Of course, its the mildest of Hock and comes from Worms, but it went to his head, and he must have got the idea it was Italian wine, because he sat straight down and wrote this, this one I've been reading you. Then he went to bed in an exalted state.'

He paused for a moment, drank my wine, and continued: 'In the morning, of course, he had a head like a punch-ball. But he remembered it was the closing date of the competition, so he asked his mother to send in the poem for him and perhaps the thought of its inevitable success helped his hangover. Anyway, by 6.30 the ceiling had settled back into place, and all those shapes and faces you see in ceilings if you look long enough had ceased to caper. So he got up.

'And the first thing that met his eye was the manuscript of the prize poem. Of course, his mother had forgotten it; and the competition was closed, the little magazines still barred to him. He went out onto the landing, to shout curses at his mother, downstairs among her culinary smells. I don't know what happened — he was still unsteady, and I suppose he tripped. He heard the handrail crack, and saw for a split second the linoleum, rushing to meet him with its uncompromising pattern. He broke his neck.

'Well, he won the competition — with the poem I read you, the villanelle he wrote when he was tight. His mother had sent it up instead of his prize poem, by mistake. Of course, if he hadn't got drunk, he wouldn't have broken his neck: but if he hadn't got drunk, he wouldn't have written the poem, you see, and it wouldn't have won.' He stopped speaking.

'Where did you hear this?' I asked: 'What was the man's name?' 'I didn't think of his name,' he answered, 'only of the story,' and he went away without paying. I saw his black and yellow head swaying among the crowd thronging the cobbles in the cool of the day. He was as drunk as his hero.

[The quotation is from Douglas's own 'Villanelle of Gorizia,' written in 1937.]

The Angel
(THE CHERWELL, 27 April 1940)

Just as darkness came across the land on the day of Michael, an angel stood over the white monastery which is on top of the hill above Gorizia. From where he stood he could see the pale green stream of Isonzo, swirling in shadow by the ruined palace of the archbishop. That was to his left, and to the right Monte Nero squatted in the darkness; and he could see that, for he was a very tall angel, and he stood with his legs straddling the valley, so that one of his feet was in a vineyard by Lucinico beyond Isonzo, and the other was placed so that the little trees on Monte Calvario sprouted between his toes, tickling them pleasantly. His tunic was of purple, and in the gloom it glowed with a strange sheen beneath his cloak, the golden cloak of the Cherubim, keepers of the winds on Lemnos before the fall. He had a golden girdle, and the clasp of that was Chalcedone, and upon it was the one gaelic word which was the angel's name.

A sentry of the Alpini at the barrack gate by the river saw the gleam of his spear in the sky, five hundred feet above Monte Calvario in the clear night air. But he was a sleepy man, and he only shifted his weight from one foot to the other, and felt the edge of his little bayonet with his left hand.

In the morning a small boy knocked at the door of the monastery above Gorizia, and to the brother who opened he told the story of what he had seen from his window in the night. The monk led him inside by the hand, spoke to him kindly, and giving him an exceedingly potent pill, sent him back to his mother, who awaited him anxiously in a dirty white house on the outskirts of the town.

Coutts
(THE CHERWELL, 27 April 1940)

'Mr Coutts,' said the Porter, 'he was queer, at least all the men thought him so. And queer he was, too, slinking along the Quad like a cat all the time. He had a friend, Mr Pope and we always thought he drove Coutts mad. They lived together at the top of nine and we used to hear Coutts sobbing when Pope was on the ramp as we called it. I often said something would happen, and it did.

'One night, John, the under porter, woke me and said Coutts was in the Dean's room. When I got there, the Dean had shut himself up in a cupboard and Coutts was banging on the door. It took four of us to hold him. We shut him up in the Bursary and in the morning the Principal rang up the asylum and they came and took him away. He'd written three letters, one to the Principal, another to himself and the third to God, and when they were taking him away and he saw the Principal holding them it was as if you'd never heard a man curse before. I shall never forget it. The Principal, he put the letters away in a drawer as evidence. A dangerous thing to be responsible for shutting up a man, he said. For a time we heard regularly how he was getting on, and they said he might recover in time.

'But soon after Easter Coutts walked into the Lodge. He seemed all right but we hadn't heard of his release. "Ah, Reynolds," he said to me, "how are you? I've just called on the Principal but he wasn't in." And he slunk through the door like he used. I talked to him and sent John to the Dean who rang up the asylum. I told him about Torpids and how we'd just missed a Bump supper and he seemed quite interested. Soon two little men with brown coats and blue trousers came, and he preceded them out quite calmly. Later, the Principal found those three letters on his desk. Coutts had found them but he'd been disturbed.

'And that was all we heard of Coutts until one night after Tom had struck. John, having let out a bunch of out-college men, dashed into the Lodge with a green face. "Mr Coutts," he gasped, "he just went out." I got a torch and had a look round outside, but he must have disappeared down the High. John said there was something funny about his face. All red and boils, it was. I sent a message up to the Dean who got in touch with the asylum, and then I went to bed. The next morning I heard that Coutts was dead. Yesterday afternoon, he'd been going to have a bath and had somehow turned on only the hot water. He died of his scalds about eight-thirty. When the Principal next went to his safe, only the letter to himself was left.'

A Present for Mimi
(THE CHERWELL, 27 April 1940)

Mimi still had deep, unfathomable eyes and a figure lovely enough to bring kings to submission, though she had worked like a slave and enjoyed herself (or at least allowed most of the clientele to enjoy her), at the Café tabac au Négre de Toulouse, for five years. For five years she had sung and hurried daintily to and fro among the wine-stained tables; had brought the filets de sole maison in their luscious sauce, trimmed with mushrooms and mussels, from the hatch through which the scent of their cooking came, to André and Gaston and Noel and Jean and a hundred just as handsome. All of them loved her and shared her favours amicably. Sometimes she worked as a model, for the Négre de Toulouse is in Montparnasse, which was as verminous with artists then as now, though there were fewer Americans. And though she will have been dead some years now, her face still smiles from the wall of that café: and in the little room above it, she still reclines against the flowery wallpaper in a dull gilt frame, voluptuously stretched upon a bed which has now long fallen to dust.

She had her favourites, as you would expect. She loved Jean Leloup for his beautiful whiskers, François for his gaiety and his extravagant toasts and eulogies of her beauty. What a poet poor François would have been, if he had ever stayed sober enough to write down his declamations, or drunk enough to conceive them when he had paper before him. He preferred Mimi and a carafe of Rosé or Beaujolais, and no one blamed him. But Mimi was ready to be in love with any of them for an afternoon or a summer evening. Then she would walk arm-in-arm with them over the cobbled street, where the gas lamp gave whiter beauty to her face for a moment against the darkness, and her bosom in its flimsy blouse glimmered until a man's black figure hid it. Often at nights the street was full of their laughter for they laughed loudly and called back to others behind them. They were young. Mimi did truly love them all, and each of them severally, so long as he had some glint of masculine attraction.

Vincent had none. He was ugly, but not in a pleasing way, and he was so gloomy. He seldom spoke, but drank and looked about him sadly. He knew he was ugly. That evening most of the others were out in the square, where the Rodin statue is now, listening to a speech. Vincent sat alone in the café except for a man in a broad hat whom nobody knew. Vincent asked for a half carafe of vin rosé and Mimi brought it. She felt lonely and even had time to be sorry for Vincent, sitting there as gloomy as ever. She sat lightly on his knee and put an arm on his shoulder and asked him to be a little gay. He told her he had painted all day and it was no good. He had painted a tree outside the window, 'and all the time the tree laughed at me. The leaves made faces and derisive expressions at me. The tree knew quite well I could not paint it. I tried to reproduce it, the way it jeered at me — but I couldn't, it has beaten me.' Mimi could not fathom this, she only laughed and said: 'Poor Vincent.' He looked up at her with his little reddish eyes, and put his hand over her breast: he thought for the hundredth time how futile was his effort to paint or make anything good, when in this simple form under his hand was contained the whole of beauty and pleasure. But if he were to love Mimi for her beautiful breasts, to fall down and worship her even, she would only laugh at him, would make a fool out of him, like the English lady, when he had worked at the art dealer's in London. So he stared past her and through her with increased heaviness. What pleasure should God take, to create such beauty as Mimi, and such perfection as Mimi's breasts, only to make his misery more huge and endless. To the others, who did not sense one half of any beauty, animals, Mimi was always free; but as for him, Vincent, who alone could realise to the full her perfection, he was forbidden her delights.

Mimi had been speaking to him, but he had not heard her. Now he heard her say: '— and I have only the one old blouse and the ugly old skirt, Vincent, will you not buy me another blouse ——', her hand moved lightly over his stubbly red hair, like a bird over a field of coarse grass, and she stroked his ear with her small fingers. 'I'm sure you would choose me a lovely blouse, Vincent.' 'I have no money,' said Vincent, 'I never have money,' he repeated lugubriously. Mimi laughed again, embarrassed by his misery, and tired of him, for the others were coming in by ones and twos and calling to her. She gave his ear a little pull: 'Never mind, Vincent,' she said, 'Look what beautiful ears you have, so fine and large, like an elephant's. Perhaps next time you see me, you will have sold a picture. You will be rich, Vincent.' And she ran across and sat down among the others.

They asked her why she had taken notice of that sour old vegetable, and she complained of their desertion and looked so pitiful that a dozen penitent moustachios instantly brushed her cheek, and she was happy again. She sipped Gaston's wine, and sang to them all, and danced with most of them, and they all went out together into the street, very boisterous and happy. They went to other cafés and drank vermouth and absinthe and a lot of coffee, and at last Mimi and Gaston slipped away from the others who were busy with a chorus and becoming a little indefinite about numbers, anyway. They walked slowly and closely linked by Gaston's long arm and Mimi's little rounded one. Every few yards they stopped in the darkest places for kisses, and when there was anywhere to sit, they sat there, under the full moon which regarded Paris quietly. Other lovers passed them, and did not look at them, nor they at those who passed. Gaston was an accomplished lover, and led Mimi through every stage of amorous occupation, contriving, as he always did, to seem like a surprised explorer, though he knew the way well. She relaxed in his arms and was quite content and very kind to him.

Gradually they made their way back to the sign of the Negro of Toulouse. Mimi unlocked the door and they came in quietly, but not stealthily, for the old woman and her husband were used to Mimi's ways, though they were angry enough if she woke them up. In the little room upstairs Mimi lit the gas and surveyed herself in the peculiar mirror. Behind her Gaston grunted, not too pleased. 'What is the matter, darling?' asked Mimi. 'Another of your admirers has seen fit to send you a present,' said Gaston. 'I shall go out again and find you a better one.' 'Don't be silly. You can't possibly get anything now. But you may buy me the ring with a little face on it, in the window opposite, tomorrow morning, my sweet.' She was busy undoing the wrappings. Inside the first of them was a note in clumsy script— 'A present for Mimi.' Inside the second wrapping was Vincent's right ear, so fine and large, like an elephant's.

The Gnome
(THE CHERWELL, 4 May 1940)
By Peter Hatred

Old Mr Latimer would not believe in the story. Brinklow, he said, was an inveterate liar and a damned truculent fellow whom he would have sacked long ago if he hadn't such an understanding of flowers. As for the second housemaid, what could you expect of a hysterical child of fifteen, given to tears and breaking plates? It was plain she had got her story from Brinklow, or the postman, who would say anything rather than stop talking and go about his business. Old Mr Latimer had never heard such fairytale foolery. This was what came of living in a poky hole like Brand, he told the vicar tactlessly, among a community of superstitious rustics whom no one bothered to educate. Ordinarily he would have gone on indefinitely about the half-witted state of the parish, emphasising his opinions in the dust with his polished and silvered cane. But now he was too annoyed. Was it not sufficient, he asked Mrs La Pole, that they should come and spoil his Christmas with their traditional peaking and piping, and wanting an exorbitant dole before they would take themselves off? They should have been content with that, without spreading cranky tales about his estate. They'd be saying there was a ghost in Rascals before they were done.

But the rumour persisted with the weeks and grew with the months. In the summer it was corroborated by two hikers whom Mr Latimer immediately had arrested for trespassing. And before the cold weather was fairly started, Sergeant Bundle and the constables from Brand and Midingham set out across old Mr Latimer's estate with his crusty permission to investigate and scotch the rumour. Old Mr Latimer watched them go off, crunching with their regulation steps over the golden and auburn leaves, and blowing out clouds of their official breath upon the sharp morning.

That evening Sergeant Bundle, showing some traces of human excitement, but in a restrained and formal manner, informed Mr Latimer that he and his constables had witnessed the truth of the rumour. 'As far as we could ascertain,' said Sergeant Bundle carefully, 'it would appear to be a species of gnome or goblin.' Old Mr Latimer, who was at his dinner, seemed very disturbed. He snapped the spindly stem of his wineglass and ate no more that evening.

From that moment the entire resources of the village were devoted to the gnome's discovery and capture. Constables with handcuffs and truncheons, the lads of the village with nets and rattles, and Slin Tapply the ex-gamekeeper with his bottle, set out to harass the fairy. Nor was it a local affair for long. The reporters and the Psychic Research Society were on the scene in no time at all. Special trains and buses began to run to Brand, though Mr Latimer allowed as few people as he could help to pass his fences. He persevered in his unbelief, while the rest of the village enjoyed the notoriety which secured Sergeant Bundle a columnsworth of interview in more than one paper. Old Mr Latimer wrote to *The Times* casting reckless aspersions upon the sobriety and veracity of almost everyone in Brand. The fact that *The Times*, true to its policy of avoiding the sensational, had ignored the gnome, and ignored his letter, did nothing to improve his temper.

The gnome continued to be seen from time to time, and kept the interest of the public, who expected every day his capture and interrogation, or like Mr Latimer would not believe in such a creature.

*   *   *

Late on Christmas Eve, Sergeant Bundle, divested of his boots of office, sat in a contented stupor before his cottage fire, busy with a large measure of mulled ale. The knocking which at first he feared came from inside his head was finally traced to the door, which he opened. Slin Tapply was outside, waving his bottle excitedly in the darkness. 'You'd better Be Off Ome,' said the sergeant with difficulty, 'else I shall 'ave to Take You In. Drunk, you are.'

'Drunk,' said Slin: 'I been drunk three weeks. Every morning I wake up drunker'n I went to sleep. You want to 'ave some of my bottle. That's what you want. I know, I know. Born in Wat's Barn I was, Midsummer Night. And I don't 'ave no respect, not for 'is 'ighness the King I don't. I got a 'undred pounds. Tucked away. I don't 'ave no respect not for old Mr Lartimer 'imself. 'E wouldn't believe me. I told 'un. I know. I told 'ole Mr Lartimer,' Slin paused to pay attention to his bottle. ' 'Ere,' said the sergeant, 'you told 'im what?' 'I bloodywell told 'un where Goblin lives. I says, what I says, 'e's livin' on Private land, I says. If it was public, anyone could go on it. But ole Mr Lartimer's land, private, that is. You carn go on it. No more no goblin carn go on it.' 'Where is 'e?'

asked the sergeant as soon as he could get a word in. 'In a little 'ole,' Slin said. 'Dug 'imself a little 'ole. Lek a little cony, I says. Carn see no more where 'e goes in nor where 'e comes out.'

Some time during the summer when the nights were warm, the gnome must have excavated that hole in the bank, entered by means of a hollow tree many hundred years old. He had not displaced the moss, and the long grass and leaves concealed what was inside. The bank was some three feet high, embracing with its green the old tree's body. Under Slin's tipsy guidance they did not find it till dawn. And in the morning, as the first bells of Christmas began to make merry, a crowd of some twenty villagers had collected there, and were talking in low voices, looking one after another at the small entrance which concealed the gnome. The crowd grew rapidly, and presently a noisier crew armed with rattles and hunting horns approached and stood round the gnome's hollow, requiring him to emerge, with the authoritative accent of aristocracy.

After about a quarter of an hour the sound of sneezing came from inside the bank, and the gnome came out. He was about three feet in height, an old gnome, peering shortsightedly. He seemed puzzled as he blinked at them: they had woken him up. They rushed towards him, but he was dead before anyone touched him.

Old Mr Latimer stood high upon the bank above them. The smoke of his gun drifted away in a compact little cloud. 'Be off with you, d'you hear?' he said furiously. 'Get off my land. I don't believe in fairies and I'll have no damn fairies on my estate.' As they went away they could hear him still raging over the corpse of the Gnome.

Rejoice in the Lamb
(THE CHERWELL, 4 May 1940)

About the year 1759 a brilliant young scholar of Cambridge University, as so many brilliant young scholars of so many universities, had finished living on the credit of his early years, and ruined bodily and mentally by an unhealthy surfeit of drink and religion was admitted to a madhouse. Here no longer young or promising, yet in his maddest minutes remembering with pain his lapse from grace, Christopher Smart suffered some four years. He was never chained or denied the light of day: he read the papers and enjoyed the society of his cat. But he was consumed with misery most of his time. The first twenty-five years of his life were almost uniformly successful. He was the son of Lord Vane's steward and on his father's death was brought up as one of His Lordship's family; in which there was a daughter of his own age, Lady Ann Vane, who was to charm Calcutta in the days of Warren Hastings. He ran away with her before either of them was fourteen, but their match 'was, however, timely prevented,' and Christopher was equipped with the traditional inspiration of poets, a hopeless love. The Lady Ann still occupied his thoughts when after a less romantic marriage he entered the asylum. His education had culminated in a fellowship at Cambridge: whose many drinking houses became his downfall.

'At college he soon acquired celebrity as a poet and wit, and according to a vicious system which ruined many men of talent, it became a custom for strangers as well as friends to invite him to taverns, that he might gratify a vulgar curiosity by displaying himself and his talents and that his entertainers might be able to boast of having been in his company. The practice was fatal to his pecuniary resources, for his pride was such that he could not accept of treats without giving treats in return, and he thus became involved in difficulties from which he never afterwards got free.' His erratic course was noted by the sober eye of Thomas Gray, not as yet famous for his Elegy; who wrote: '. . . all this, you see, must come to a Jayl, or Bedlam, and that without any help, almost without pity.'

Gray's words like those of many righteous and gloomy prophets, were fulfilled; and Christopher Smart descending from a fellowship to hack journalism and thence to the madhouse, emerged only in 1763 to publish 'A Song of David': which though his fame now rests upon it, moved many to say that he should never have been allowed out.

But during his years of confinement he was occupied in writing a much stranger and perhaps a greater poem, in lines of wandering prose, sometimes similar to the English of the psalms, and recording his own past and present life, many events of the day, and much miscellaneous learning. The whole is unified by the strain of what seems insanity running through it. My idea in writing this short essay, is to bring to notice this poem, which though it has now been published, has not received much attention from ordinary readers. And after this introduction the best I can do is to quote from it, since nothing else will give a right impression of its amazing nature.

It begins with a hymn of praise more or less in the Hebrew idiom: which proceeds from

> Rejoice in God, O ye tongues. Give glory to the Lord, and the Lamb.
> Let Noah and his company approach the Throne of Grace, and do homage to the Ark of their Salvation.

to

> Let Moses, the man of God, bless with a Lizard, in the sweet majesty of goodnature, and the magnanimity of meekness.

and further still

> Let Ethan praise with the Flea, his coat of mail, his piercer, and his vigour, which wisdom and providence have contrived to attract observation and to escape it.
> Let Heman bless with the Spider, his warp and his woof, his subtlety and industry, which are good.
> Let Chalcol praise with the Beetle, whose life is precious in the sight of God, though his appearance is against him.

From these extravagant praises he proceeds to immense depths of learning, often in Natural History,

> Let Arodi rejoice with the Royston Crow, there is a society of them at Trumpington and Cambridge.
> Let Naomi rejoice with Pseudosphece, who is between a wasp and a hornet.
> Let Manoah rejoice with Cerastes, who is a dragon with horns.
> Let Abigail rejoice with the Lethophagus God be gracious to the widows indeed.

He will presently speak of himself, 'For I am not without authority in my jeopardy' and he says

> For I meditate the Peace of Europe amongst family bickerings and Domestic jars
> For I bless the Prince of Peace and pray that all the guns may be nailed up, save such as are for rejoicing days.

His meditation continues between sanity and madness, arousing laughter sometimes, sympathy, and respect. From the height of sublimity he falls to what may seem at first pathetic and absurd, though sincerity should justify it:

> For I bless God for the postmaster General and all Con-
> veyancers of letters especially Allen and Shelvock.
> For I have seen the White Raven and Thomas Hall of Willing-
> ham and am myself a greater curiosity than both.

This is more than enough of quotation but before I end, the completest and finest poem I have ever seen about a cat must be put down here, lest these extracts are still to be all you see of 'Rejoice in the Lamb.'

> For I am possessed of a cat, surpassing in beauty, from whom I
> take occasion to bless Almighty God. . . .
> For at the first glance of the Glory of God in the East he
> worships in his way. . . .
> For having considered God and himself he will consider his
> neighbour.
> For if he meets another cat he will kiss her in kindness.
> For when he takes his prey he plays with it to give it a chance.
> For one mouse in seven escapes by his dallying.
> For he is of the Lord's poor and so indeed is he called by
> benevolence perpetually — Poor Jeoffrey! Poor Jeoffrey! The
> rat has bit thy throat.
> For I bless the name of the Lord Jesus that Jeoffrey is better.
> For the divine spirit comes about his body to sustain it in
> compleat cat.
> For his tongue is exceeding pure so that it has in purity what it
> wants in music.
> For he is docile and can learn certain things.
> For he can jump from an eminence into his master's bosom.
> For he can catch the cork and toss it again.
> For by stroaking of him I have found out electricity.
> For though he cannot fly, he is an excellent clamberer.
> For he can swim for life.
> For he can creep.

There is more even of this part than I can quote. But perhaps here is enough to interest you. The whole poem is what is usually called a human document, and presents in its entirety the picture of the kind and pitiful person who wrote it. It is particularly interesting because it is a diary, not written for anyone else to read, and so its poetry is personal and completely sincere; as no poetry can ever quite succeed to be, which is written for the perusal of others.

Published by Jon. Cape, ed. W. F. Stead.   K.

The Poetry of James Henry Leigh Hunt
(THE CHERWELL, 1 June 1940)
By John Oligarch

Leigh Hunt was not a successful, or great poet, because he was narrow in his ideal of poetry, which was, as he says, to convey to the rest of the world his pleasure at some example of beauty, flowers or a heroic narrative. He wanted to reproduce the picture of these things, perhaps a little more vividly: to colour the hyacinth or the sunlight with his own enthusiasm. And reproduction of a picture in words was the largest thing he sought.

His author's preface to the edition of 1832 is an explanation of almost all his success and failure as a poet. He says of poetry:

> in its highest sense (it) belongs exclusively to such men as Shakespere, Spenser, and others who possessed the deepest insight into the spirit and sympathies of all things; but poetry, in the most comprehensive application of the term, I take to be the flower of any kind of experience, rooted in truth, and issuing forth into beauty.

And this is a competent and beautiful definition, but what he says elsewhere in this preface shows that he interpreted the flower of experience issuing forth to be experience itself. And his poetry recounts experience without drawing any conclusion.

It is true that he employed verse to give vent to his political opinions, but he himself would not have claimed for these works of 'Leigh Hunt at his most unbuttoned' the title of poetry. In consideration of his poetry, his political satires are only worthy of mention to save their confusion with his poetry proper, which we take to mean his narratives in verse, his plays, his short serious verses and translations, with perhaps his imitations grudgingly admitted.

For imitation together with an attendant sense of formula is another fetter of his poetry. Milford ignores the *Juvenilia* which Hunt published in 1801 at the age of sixteen, as being 'almost wholly worthless.' As judgment of their poetic content, this stands. But they may help towards understanding Hunt's poetry.

The *Juvenilia* show a fatal competence in versification, already a professional polish at the tender age of twelve, in the poem Macbeth; in which every vestige of inspiration is absent, perhaps stamped out by Boyer's methods. Nothing which may be called

really original appears until about a quarter of the way through
the book, which we suppose to be chronologically arranged, in
the poem, 'Lines on the Birthday of Eliza,' where in the not very
original lines

> So softly shakes her fluttering hair,
> While in its silken locks the breeze
> Entwining sports with playful ease

he does achieve some freshness and appear interested. A few
poems later comes the 'Description of a morning's walk and
view,' perhaps inspired by Hunt's holiday in the country, upon
which Christ's Hospital insisted for each boy once during his
schooldays. Here, as indeed in every poem of his, there is a
continual use of clichés, but some good lines begin to appear,
recording a good bit of personal observation; though 'the vig'rous
heifer, pity-bleating calf' is very unpleasant. Leigh Hunt never
became so involved in this type of poetic diction as other minor
poets of his age. In R.D. Blackmore's translation of *Vergil's
Eclogues*, for instance (which as a translation is more wandering
than most), the words cattle, cow, and shepherd are never used,
beeves, heifer, and swain being substituted, though such strange
language is not thought necessary in *Lorna Doone*.

Leigh Hunt also suffered from the necessity for hack-writing,
and much of his verse has a journalistic quality: some is very poor
doggerel. He could not work into his poetry any of his political
convictions, for where they appear his verse is straightway dried
up with prosaic and parliamentary terms. But his love of the
country, beauty, and heroism; and his contempt for family
tyranny; in fact his kindly and romantic character does appear in
his poems. His ideal of technique is however harder to come at
than his ideal of matter. He praises Shakespeare for speaking of
moonlight 'sleeping' on a bank, or Milton for describing flowers
'bosomed' in trees — but that he himself should lapse from
conventionality into what he calls animal spirits, is matter for
apology; which he makes, for writing of a ship 'swirling' into
harbour. His poetic education must have smothered his poetic
instinct.

Yet there are many memorable lines in his poetry as those in
'The Story of Rimini': 'with heaved out tapestry the windows
glow' and

> Hark! The approaching trumpets with a start
> On the smooth wind come dancing to the heart.

Those powers of description which make his essays remarkable adorn his poetry no less,when in such lines as those 'To the White Rose of America,' he speaks of his beloved flowers —

> The bright sunflower's top of burnished gold,
> The yellow jonquil, varicoloured pink —
> The purple Passion-flower —

He even thinks a footnote necessary on the Passion Flower.

But a poet must draw conclusions. Hunt could only point like a more clumsy Aesop one or two obvious morals, tacked on to the song's tail. Though he carefully pruned and edited his huge and too prolific store of verse, and though he could write lines like these, echoed in John Drinkwater's 'God of Quiet,'

> Proud city, that by the Ligurian sea
> Sittest, as at a mirror, lofty and fair,

Leigh Hunt only produced two poems valuable as a whole: the famous 'Abou ben Adhem,' and the rondeau, 'Jenny kissed me.'

This is because he never seems to have set out to make a poem with the derivation of the word in mind: a thing made, done, perfect, complete in itself. There are few of his to which he could not have added another hundred lines when the spirit moved him.

The Happy Fatalist
(THE CHERWELL, 1 June 1940)

The happiest person at such times is presumably the fatalist [Dunkirk had been evacuated on 26 May]: what he loses in the enjoyment of high hopes he gains in immunity from despair. The advantages of his philosophy are still more those of freedom from panic and the ability to be unprejudiced by what has happened, what is happening, and what will happen. There may be those (apparently there are) who can still believe in God as a benevolent divine uncle: and by all means let each find comfort where his reason allows him. But even for the fatalist the facts of good and evil remain, and he should be able to appreciate them better than anyone else.

For he is not that hopeless castaway he sometimes appears, he does not trust in nothing, nor is he faithless. He rather believes in the most evident and omnipotent deity of all, whose ways are not inscrutable, who moves in a wonderful but not a mysterious way, and who is as fundamentally just as any other deity has ever been. To some the fatalist may still seem to be cold and inhuman, and as far as reason and impartiality are not the true characteristics of humanity, he is inhuman, and superhuman.

Happy fatalists can listen to the news and the rumours and enjoy in spite of them the occasions which even war cannot make less pleasant. Here at least there is still pleasure and activity for a good many people, and it would be foolish to let any forboding spoil either. [. . .]

No Cuddling
(THE CHERWELL, 8 June 1940)

We might ignore Beverley Nichols' maiden-avuncular criticisms [he had attacked undergraduates in a Sunday newspaper]; it can cause us no anxiety that he should condemn us, though his praise would indeed mark us down. But there is evidently a considerable force of opinion independent of, though now perhaps fanned by, Nichols, which holds that Oxford is the home exclusively of totally exempt conscientious objectors, that we callously ignore the sufferings even of those who a few months ago stood here with us, and almost that we are responsible for the disaster in France and Belgium. An undergraduate's mother writes to him:

'It was thinking of these things that made me feel rather hysterical when I read your letter saying you had found another strange-looking female to go about with and are continuing your course of work "as though there were no war." I realised suddenly that you were just one of hundreds still living like that, many blaming — and justly blaming — the older generation for not being more prepared, but nevertheless not willing to go to a ha'porth of trouble to try and make things any better. Not giving one sou or one hour of leisure to anyone but themselves. If hundreds at Oxford and other universities had been less apathetic we should have been more ready for invasion now.'

It is not difficult to see how easily this point of view, expressed by someone who though reasonably minded is quite out of touch with Oxford and with the War, will appeal to the fraternity of Blimps and will further incense the workers of the world with the idea that Undergraduates Can Do Anything They Like. The accusation is based in general on the fact that Oxford is endeavouring to carry on as a university with a personnel for eighty per cent of whom a call up is imminent. The letter was written to an undergraduate who has at the most until July. In particular it is prompted by the fact that he had written saying his tutor had urged him to defeat the war as long as possible by refusing to adjust his scheme of work to it day by day; and describing a new girl friend. This is to imply then, in general, that Oxford should pass at least temporarily out of existence, and that bands of undergraduates should rush to offer their services to the government. And in particular, that This is No Time For Cuddling, and any patriotic student will leave his work and join one of those semi-civilian organisations for wasting taxpayers' money of which there are now so many. Let us look carefully and see what good this could do. In the first place almost every undergraduate is registered already for one or more forms of national service: several wait up at night to greet hypothetical I.R.A. men with fifteen rounds of ball and a bayonet: farming and forestry schemes will occupy numbers of those who are not absorbed into the services during the long vacation. Any further activity would probably be discouraged. And in any case most of us might be allowed some amusement during the last few weeks we are able to get it. Moreover, a great part of the conscientious objectors will be doing work with ambulances a good deal more dangerous than that of several patriotic heroes who joined up at the outbreak of war to do office work in uniform.

These are the present and future activities of this town of lotus eaters: and besides all this we have up to now preserved a sufficient part of the essential university, have kept the love of learning, a reasonable outlook, and the importance of ordinary things alive, many of the blessings of peace which have elsewhere departed. Our critics outside will probably not concede that there is any use in preserving a university magazine which treats of such shocking subjects as the decadence of the eighteen nineties at this stern season: or in encouraging wittiness at the Union, or in performing plays and good music. These are the dissipations of the intelligent, and the unintelligent prudently condemn them, for theirs is a powerful voice and if they can stamp such things out, no one will know any more that they are unintelligent. But perhaps even they will admit there is some use in the continuation to prune the various branches of learning and art, and for all our apathy both still flourish here.

There is further the accusation that if we had been less apathetic in the past we should have been more ready for invasion now. It is hard to see the very smallest evidence of reasoning or justification behind this amazing statement. If the government were largely composed of undergraduates or even of Dons: if it were even aware of the fact, that some undergraduates are sensible, and if it were eager to take their advice on major points of policy, then we might bear the accusation of apathy with justice. But in this curiously arranged country, everyone is legally a zany until he is twenty-one. A man may be taken away and blown up at an age when he is not allowed to lead an independent life in his spare time. All we are permitted to do is further to show our youthful foolishness by writing our names under offers of service to the government of our elders — not even in sarcasm can we bring ourselves to add — 'and betters'. This signature we have most of us completed. But for some time yet we shall continue to hear the slurs cast upon us, until the chances of war have made many more of us deaf to them. The thought that we shall fight to save these futile critics so that their futile criticism may outlive us is one of the greatest burdens and discouragements we have to bear.

During his second year at Oxford Douglas spent as little time with fellow writers as during his first. *The Cherwell*, however, had become as much an organ for his poetry as for his journalism and prose. His co-editing of *Augury* further established the reputation which was to lead the generation of undergraduate writers immediately following his own, Sidney Keyes, John Heath-Stubbs and Michael Meyer among them, to include his work in their *Eight Oxford Poets*. Douglas had spent much of the Easter vacation 1940 selecting and typing up his poems with a view to publishing a collection. In the summer term he passed them to Blunden.

21 May 1940   *Merton College*

My dear Keith, I restore your MSS., no, TSS. with the assurance that you have here produced a most attractive series of poems, interesting alike in the way you think about things, the painter's

quality in the treatment, and the originality with which you vary
normal metres. You will find a very few pencil markings on the
pages; so far as I can judge there is scarcely any item which it
would be best to exclude, the vitality of eager feeling and shaping
seems to me to be present in nearly all.

But now, what is to be done? Will you send the MS. up to a
publisher? it is a ghoulish moment for such matters, but possibly
publishers are less afflicted with MSS. than in normal times. I
would suggest (1) J. Cape or (2) Faber. With Mr Hart-Davis of
Cape I have an ancient friendship, and can speak to him of you
and your work, — but I have no real contact with Faber, and
indeed my name *there* might only cause Mr Eliot (who perhaps
'reads' for the firm) to suspect you were in some sort of my
poetical platoon, and do nothing.

Let me thank you on my own account as a reader for the
pleasure and quickening your verse gives me, and this is
naturally all the better to reflect upon in view of our old C.H. We
have had some pretty good poets, Peele, Coleridge, Lamb, Hunt,
but the line must be extended! and I think you can do it.

Yours ever, *EB*

[*June 1940*]   *Hadlow House Nr Uckfield, Sussex*

Dear E.B. I'm not to report for a week or 2, so I shall have time to
clear things up a bit. My poems are packed up and in transit here
by goods, with the rest of my stuff — but when they come I think I
shall send them to you for safe keeping, and if at any time you
think it worth while handing the[m] over to J. Cape please do so
and I will write them a letter from wherever I am at the moment.
Meanwhile I am going down to Housey to get as much riding as
possible before I actually get to the cavalry, and to learn up
Cavalry training and Horsemastership.

Love to Sylva   In haste *Keith*

Do you know Hamo Sasson's address?

[*June/July 1940*]   *Marlhurst, Southwater, Sussex*

Dear E.B. Thank you for your card — I am as you guessed more or
less at Housey by now. I got out at C.H. Station yesterday

evening and walked up through the serried ranks of the corps to the shop, where I took an innocent drink before walking back to Southwater. I met Mr Buck who seems very well, and asked after you.

I am likely to have at least one ride per day while I'm here and shall spend most of the rest of my time hanging about the shop, unless the Head chases me off.

Thank you for accepting the protection of my poems — I'll send them you as soon as I get back to Hadlow Down. I doubt if I shall write any more for some time — I am now trying to learn cavalry Training and the Manual of Horsemastership by heart. Already I know that the horse has a very small stomach, which I never expected, and that he requires from 5–15 gallons of water a day. I never met one that took anywhere near the 15. I suppose he would be regarded with awe by his companions as a 7 bucket-man.

I must stop now, as I want to catch Mr Roberts before he comes out of school and makes for Horsham.

Best wishes to you and Sylva   *Keith*

[July 1940]

Dear Edmund, I'm afraid I have to cancel the dinner engagement for tomorrow night, as I've been called up and have to go to Edinburgh (I think) immediatley. I'll let you know further developments. I'm so sorry.

In haste   *Keith*

On 7 July 1940 Douglas reported to Redford Barracks, Edinburgh and remained there two months as cavalry trooper. During September/October he was in the last group to train at the Army Equitation School, Weedon. From there he moved to the mechanized Wing at Sandhurst, training as Officer Cadet until January 1941.

15 October 1940   *Merton College*

My dear Keith, This delay is lamentable but I have been variously lazy or busy — I am at all events glad I do not have to polish butt plates of rifles, in spite of which task you have written some fine poems. It is not much good *my* praising you, for I am considered antediluvian, but I'll say the two you sent me ['The News from Earth' and 'An Oration'], in different ways, are the best verse I've seen lately outside the Old Masters. In time, these admirable unions of wise humanity and strong fancy will be properly appreciated.

No news. There is to be a 'Cherwell', a Bach Choir, a Change Ringers Society and an English Club. The lads are dining in hall with proper veneration. Some live in the heavy construction on Rose Lane, and will probably come out all spots like the former occupants of the Maginot Line.

Two C.H. girls graced my room, or rather Father Williams's room, where your watercolour is exhibited, yesterday afternoon. I hope the latest London church to be bombed is not Christ Church, Newgate St. It will be sad if that marvellous living remembrancer of S.T.C., C.L., L.H. and so many more should be at last destroyed in this fantastic aberration.

I can only hope that you will write presently new 'Memoirs of a Cavalier' in a spirit of great cheerfulness, though also of farewell to the neighing steed. (Othello I take it was of the Infantry, Artillery, Engineers, Cavalry, and several special corps.)

But now I must leave you to borrow some soldiers friend. Usual dialogue in our Canteen late 1916:

Honest Soldier. 'Got any tinned stuff, Trew?'

Trew. 'No, only tholdier'th friend.'

Best luck. Do you hear any aircraft about? It seems to me —

Yours ever *EB*

16 December 1940   *Merton College*

The Works have gone off to T. S. Eliot, including the latest pieces: I have sent all that were in my hands. As for 'Spectator', I should say, send any new things if you like, as you produce them. The Lit. Editor is Graham Greene and the address 99 Gower Street London W.C.1. I have been pretty busy especially with the scholarship examinations, and expect you are with all sorts of activities. Sorry I was not on the scene when you came last. The *Cherwell* appears to have upset one or two dignitaries, but has been well done, — I expect the editorship is to be transferred next term. Of other Journals I know nothing at the moment, the one which Dr Marie Stopes befriends is said to be in need of a new cover design. Best Luck, and to Hamo if with you. *EB*

🍂

The journal referred to was *Kingdom Come*. Douglas sent a design of an angel in the midst of war's machinery: 'This was to have been my Christmas Card, if I'd had the time to make one'.

🍂

16 December 1940   *Merton College*

Dear Eliot, I was sorry that the plan you so kindly proposed to me for publishing a selection from my poems was not acceptable to Messrs. Macmillan, whose decision I felt was binding on me and natural in them. (They are about to issue my second volume of collected pieces, and they mention the possibility of *their* ultimately producing a selection of all.) I was really pleased that you should have thought of me for a moment in this connection.

One of our Oxford poets, who has been in the Army for some time now, asked me to submit his work to you for possible publication. He had a considerable reputation here alike as a writer and an artist, so I hope you will not find it totally uninteresting to glance at what he offers. As he is at the

Royal Military College,
Camberley,
Surrey,

perhaps any communication on the subject might most con- veniently be sent to him there, should there be anything —.

But I apologize for adding to what must be a cascade of poetical applications always being made to you.

[*Edmund Blunden*]

[*January 1941*]   *33 Tp.B. Sqn. Royal Armoured Wing, R.M.C.*

Dear Edmund, Thank you for the card — I hope the Great man doesn't lose the poems — I've lost all other copies of some of them. The party is to be on January 21st (Saturday) from 5.0 onwards. Birthday presents *in the form of bottles* will be gratefully received. We are having some difficulty in finding anywhere to hold this gathering, but when we do I'll let you know. Will Silva and your daughter come too? And if your daughter can produce any good looking and brilliant conversationalists from Somerville they will be most welcome. Over to you . . . *Keith*

19 January 1941 *Merton College*

The great man has made no sign, though I gave him your address in case he preferred to go into the matter direct with the author. Meanwhile thank you for the new Pieces, which I will keep here safely, and in time you'll be reclaiming them for a grand new Muster. We look forward to the visit and celebration which you spoke of. Please forgive this short note. Some of the old hands are back again, pacing rather sadly through the snow — and anyway some day we'll sing Diffugere nives — *EB*

To T. S. ELIOT
26 January 1941 *Merton College*

I am asked by the young writer of the collection of Poems which by his desire I submitted a few weeks ago to say that he is about to be transferred to another unit and his address will be:
K. C. Douglas (2Lt.), C/o G.P.O., Ripon
If he could have a decision he'd be grateful, for naturally he feels that his near future is liable to sudden move. With best respects
    Yours sincerely   *E. Blunden*

Eliot wrote to Blunden on 6 February saying that he found promise in the poems, and perhaps more, but did not think the collection ripe for publication. He was also slightly concerned that he was more impressed by some of the earlier poems than by more recent ones. He asked Blunden whether he had the same impression, said he was glad that he had sent the poems and thought the author should be encouraged.

To T. S. ELIOT
10 February 1941   Merton College

Best thanks for your letter, and all the trouble you have taken
over K. Douglas. I am sure anything you tell him will be carefully
thought over by him, and will help to correct the effects of his
rather too ready ways into print here. (He was in most of the best
periodicals etc. and perhaps grew too fluent.) I am sorry to hear
you have been ill and wish you may find an early and sturdy
Spring now in Surrey for a good recovery. Am not really powerful myself, it is true [. . .]

   Yours sincerely   E. Blunden

15 February 1941

Dear Mr Douglas, I have been somewhat delayed by illness in
considering your poems which Mr Blunden sent me some time
ago, but I have now read them several times and with continued
interest.

   They seem to me extremely promising, and I should like to
keep in touch with you. I should much like to know whether
circumstances permit you to keep on writing at the present, or
whether we must expect a silence of indefinite duration.

   My impression so far is that you have completed one phase
which begins with the very accomplished juvenilia and that you
have started on another which you have not yet mastered. Of the
first phase I feel that, as might be expected, there is a certain
musical monotony in the rhythms. That does not matter in itself
because it is a good thing to go on doing one thing until you are
sure that its use is exhausted. . . . I think you have definitely an
ear.

   What I should like to see is the second phase which you have
begun developed to the point of formal mastery, and meanwhile I
think it would be useful to get poems in periodicals outside of
Oxford. There are not, of course, many periodicals now in which
to publish verse, but I shall be very glad to draw the attention of
the editors of 'Horizon' to your work. If you are still writing I
should like to see something.

I am keeping the poems which Blunden gave me until I hear from you.

Yours very truly   *T. S. Eliot*

On 1 February 1941 Douglas had passed out from the Royal Military College, Sandhurst, taking up his commission with the 2nd Derbyshire Yeomanry at Ripon on 7 February. In March he moved with the regiment to Wickwar, Gloucestershire. Receiving Eliot's letter at Ripon, Douglas had responded enthusiastically in passing the news to a friend from Oxford, Jean Turner: 'Coo! I had a letter from T. S. Eliot today — quite nice on the whole — promising young man — send some more when you've written it. How much can I sell his autograph for?' Douglas replied to Eliot, asking him to return the collection to Blunden with suggestions as to which poems should be submitted to *Horizon*. Sending it in March, Eliot told Blunden that he had not meant poems from this collection because most of them, among them the best, had already been published. And he left Blunden to choose from the few remaining ones, adding the comment that Douglas did not seem to find his present circumstances conducive to writing. Blunden thanked Eliot on 13 March 1941, and returned the collection to Douglas.

[*March 1941*]   *C Sqn. 2nd Derbyshire Yeomanry, Glos.*

Dear Edmund, Thank you for your letter and the poems: I shall look through them, just to assure myself that I really used to write poetry once, and then I think if you'll consent to sit on them for me again, I'll send them back.

Do you take Eliot's letter (as I take his to me) as an excessively polite refusal to have anything to do with my efforts? I really think I give up — I may try and write a novel but I doubt it. As a poet I seem to lack the correctly exotic style and don't really get on very well with the present rulers of poetic society. I am inclined not to *destroy* my poems as yet, but another reason for returning them to you is that on impulse I am quite likely to burn them.

I hear another Augury is to be produced and wish it better success than the last, of which Basil Blackwell finally said 'Thank God we managed to get some burnt in the blitz on London.'

I am drinking much too much and gradually ceasing to think. I don't think anything will get me out of it this time — anyway my military efficiency is unimpaired, and I get on quite well with my troop who don't mind a bloated out-of-condition appearance and no epigrams.

Thank you for taking so much trouble over the poems.

Love to Silva   *Keith*

Douglas nonetheless sent Eliot four of his recent poems: 'The House', 'Song: Dotards do not think', 'The Marvel' and 'Time Eating'.

24 June 1941   *London*

Dear Mr Douglas, I have now had time to brood over your new poems and have made some marginal comments. In spite of appearances, I like the poems and I think that the one called *Song* is very nearly written. The others seem to me to need a good bit of work with special attention to ineffective adjectives. I am least certain about the one called *The House*. It is obscure and I am not sure that its myth is wholly consistent. For instance, toward the end you spoke of exorcising the dead lady in the upper room. One does speak of exorcising ghosts from material houses but in this case, the lady to be exorcised seems to be very much more substantial than the house in which you have set her. That is what I mean by inconsistency.

With best wishes.

Yours sincerely, *T. S. Eliot*

Eliot's marginal comments were fairly extensive, many of them concerned with details of phrasing: 'dim water' in 'The Marvel' elicited 'was the water dimmer than most sea water?'; 'interesting waves' was queried with 'Why?'; numerous epithets in 'The House' were questioned. (Several examples were quoted in *TLS* 2 July 1970, p.731.) Mrs Douglas sent on the letter and the annotated poems, perhaps following Eliot's advice that the remarks in his letter lost their point apart from the marginal notes. It was four months before Douglas received them. He was not enthusiastic. Eliot, he wrote to Jean Turner, 'wishes me (dear unimaginative man) to give more attention to ineffectual adjectives.' The cause of delay in receiving the letter was Douglas's posting to the Middle East. He sailed on 17 July 1941.

[?August 1941]   *Draft Serial R.W.7.K./7*

Dear Edmund, The wonders of the ocean are a little diffident but present themselves now and then; and the sun and moon have certainly been doing strange things. I have at last begun a novel but it bores me, however I'm plugging away. Unfortunately I can't manage verse as well so that is stagnant. There is very little in the line of duty and not much excitement. People are pretty boring and identical. I share this cabin with a love sick young man who uses me for a sort of confessor of which I get heartily sick. I pull his leg without compunction but it will stretch to any length apparently without his noticing. Myself, I narrowly missed being married before I left, and am very relieved still to be independent. Though I should like to think I was stinging the Pay Office for a marriage allowance.

At the moment I'm over sun burnt and very sore. But I suppose it'll pass. I force myself to do some P.T. every afternoon and so counteract to a certain extent the four huge and excellently-cooked meals a day. We get most of our entertainment (a few of us) from watching the rest. Many of my former mentors at the Equitation School provide more than most. The cryptic quality of that sentence, which I must admit reads like one of Torquemada's, is a sop to whatever Base censor may peruse this. For the moment I censor it myself, but all letters, particularly to Oxford, that home of strange foreigners, are liable to reopening.

There are occasional concerts, of the sing-song-music-hall variety, but none touch great heights, although we have on board a professional accordionist, a very good performer on the banjo, and the composer of the once celebrated Penny Serenade; (or one of the composers of it — these songs seem to be written by more and more people's collaboration, the simpler and more banal they are.)

I trust you and others to maintain the atmosphere of Oxford and the finances of Merton in a state fit for heroes to return to. If I still escape marriage I shall be back, in the flesh, or disembodied, to compete with Duns Scotus. I don't suppose we should clash much — I never could work in the library for long — and should probably spend all my time on the river, in the Ashmolean, and browsing round Blackwells, or L.M.H.

There's no news as yet for you to pass on, except that of course I'm bored, healthy, and only kept from pining away by a rumour that there are women on one of the other boats. If they're there, I wonder if the Samuel Goldwyn moonlight has the same effect on them.

Love to Sylva, and all my friends (if any). *Keith*

Many of the letters Blunden wrote Douglas over the next two years are lost. His letters to Mrs Douglas, however, do survive and through them we can trace the missing side of the triangular correspondence. The perspective is at once distorting and curiously appropriate; the two older people communicating in England; Douglas sending off his news from the Middle East to receive answers we can only guess at. The perspective is repeated in a correspondence which now opened up with J. C. Hall, all Hall's letters to Douglas being lost. In September 1941 Hall wrote to Mrs Douglas about the possibility of her son's work appearing alongside his own and that of Alan Rook in a three-man *Selected Poems*.

12 September 1941   *Merton College*

Dear Mrs Douglas, It is a puzzle indeed. My guess is that you might send Messrs Hall and Rook the collection of poems by Keith which I now pass over to you, and let them choose their 15, but on condition that Keith's consent arrives, and that the whole thing is on a business footing. For example, he should retain the rights in the poems, other than for the purposes of this book.

I had half thought you should stand aside from the project, but since T. S. Eliot decided that he could not publish K's volume I've not heard of anything promising, and so the Hall-Rook plan might be agreeable to K.

The information about the magazine appearances of some of the poems is imperfect, but what there is is shown in the collection.

Of the publication which may have been advertised in the

Cherwell I heard nothing, at least I remember nothing said.

And alas I've no address for Keith — I answered a letter from him to A.P.O. 1000 since when, nothing.

You must be greatly worried by the obscurity round his present duties, but I am sure he is equal to the occasion and perhaps is getting the experiences for his future work as artist in his several techniques.

Excuse my dullness, kindest wishes from us, and may you soon have a brilliant signal from K.

Yours sincerely, *E. Blunden*

postmark: 10 Oct 1941

[Dear Edmund,   Please excuse] the Calligraphy — I'm writing in bed in the 23rd Scottish (very Scottish) General Hospital somewhere (and having been brought here in the dark and stupor I don't know myself where) in Palestine. In Cairo (than which I never expect to find a more unsavoury habitat of more unsavoury people) I picked up some bug out of a swimming bath, which with the casual aid of the RAMC deafened me, gave me a temperature and provided more agony than I have ever had in my life. I was posted to a Regiment shortly afterwards and not wishing to be left behind I set out with the others eating Vegenin tablets in much the same way as people used to think Americans chewed gum. By the time when, in the early hours of the morning, we arrived at the particular stationless spot in the wilderness where the Regiment lives, I had run out of dope, and was therefore staggering like a drunken man and at my wits end. I spent the rest of the day with millions of flies and tons of sand, on a camp bed and in the evening set out in an ambulance for what the M.O. said would be a 2 hr drive to this hospital. How anyone unconscious stays in an army ambulance God knows. I hung on and after 3 hours by my watch, when we had stopped about 10 times I asked the driver if he had any idea where he was. After making him repeat his answers several times I found he didn't know, and it was only by sheer luck it turned out that we were already in the hospital grounds. Here I still am after, I think, about 3 weeks. I have read 32 books, 32 being all I could get, among them the works of such master writers as Ruby M. Ayres (My love came back) — this book took about ¼ of an hour to read as I was able to read a paragraph at a time, instead of, as with

Charles Morgan, a word at a time. I have consumed also many detective stories, but by rather unfair systems of deduction (I.P. by comparison with other detective stories) I usually know who dun it. However among all this I found The Fountain (C. Morgan) A Passage to India (which I'm afraid I hadn't read) Now East, Now West, S. Ertz, Les Silences du Colonel Bramble, Corduroy (A. Bell), all of which I enjoyed a lot, but most of all the Fountain, and all of which I praise almost without qualification except of type. Corduroy is rather untidy. I've found some interesting period pieces — Stella Maris by W. J. Lock with beautiful, really well-done wash illustrations — why can't we have them now — I suppose they're too expensive — and a wonderful Hodder & Stoughton paper-covered adventure called Jim goes North, about a gold-rush in Alaska, with a villain who really knows his job and is moreover called Jasper, and a sweet, innocent heroine. In the Frozen North men are not only men but Nature's Gentlemen as well. I enjoyed it a lot.

In Cairo I was forced to speak French for hours to various beautiful Eastern damsels — but it wasn't worth the effort — they are too mercenary, their parents are not at all accommodating, and I am too poor. I left Cairo with 5 piastres.

You may be interested to hear that my companion and comrade in arms (since he has been posted to the same regt.) ever since I left England is one John Masefield, a nephew of the illustrious person of that name. He is most un-literary, but an amusing chap — he spent 3 years in the Rhodesian police as a trooper, and returned to England, having his 'A' licence, under the impression that the Royal Air Force might be interested in someone who was fit and had about 100 hours flying experience. But they were very dilatory and he arrived, via the RAOC, in the Tank Corps: I see I've come to the end. My address is NOTTS. YEO. M.E.F.

Love to Sylva and Claire — *Keith*

[*October 1941*] *Cairo*

Dear Mr Eliot, If you are interested, here is the only poem I've produced since sailing from England ['Negative Information']. Life is likely to be very active from now, and I think you'd better have this while I've time to send it.

I hope it reaches you, *Keith Douglas*

Dear Edmund, I've been in hospital with a bug in my ear and now, gradually recovering, have produced one poem, which I send you. I think I sent another of these sans poem off into the blue with your name on it, last week. So in case it arrives, and because there can't be much more ink in this pen, I'll not write much now.   *Keith*

I've sent a copy of this to TSE. as he apparently wrote to my mother asking to see what I sent home. Write me an Airgraph if you've time. It'll get here in a month. Let Jon [sic] Hall have any poems he wants but please demand them back when he's finished.

Negative Information

As lines, the unrelated symbols of
nothing you know, discovered in the clouds
idly made on paper or by the feet of crowds
on sand, keep whatever meaning they have,

and you believe they write, for some
intelligence, messages of a sort;
These curious indentations on my thought
with every week, with each hour, come.

Perhaps you remember the fantastic moon
in the Atlantic — we descried the prisoner laden
with the thornbush & lantern —
the phosphorescence, the ship singing a sea-tune.

How we lost our circumstances that night
and, like spirits attendant on the ship
now at the mast, now on the waves, might almost dip
and soar, as lightly as our entranced sight.

Against that, the girls who met us at one place
were not whores, but women old & young at once
whom accidents had turned to pretty stones,
to images alight with deceptive grace.

And in general, the account of many deaths —
whose portents, which should have undone the sky,
had never come — is now received casually.
You & I are careless of these millions of wraiths,

For as often as not, we meet
in dreams our own dishevelled ghosts;
and opposite, the modest hosts
of our ambition stare them out.

To this, there's no sum I can find —
the hungry omens of calamity
mixed with good signs, & all received with levity
or indifference by the amazed mind.

16.10.41

postmark: 17 October 1941   *Notts SR Yeo MEF*

Dear John, I have sent two airgraphs which attempt to explain the
situation of my poems at the moment [the airgraphs were of the
poems 'These grasses' and 'Negative Information']. I am helpless
and if you weren't in too much of a hurry to wait for this letter, the
best I can do is to try to remember which poems I'd like to go in
and tell you to select for yourself with those in mind. My 2
airgraphs were in reply to a cable from my mother, sent as from
you. Finally she copied out your letter on an airgraph and sent
that. Well, then — I should like one or both poems called
SOISSONS to go in. VILLANELLE OF SPRING BELLS, TIME EATING,
THE MARVEL, KRISTIN, POOR MARY, STARS, CANOE, possibly EXTEN-
SION TO FRANCIS THOMPSON, under a less pretentious title,
SHADOWS, BURIAL OF A GOD, a SONG beginning, or having a verse
beginning Dotards do not think. RUSSIANS, the POEM I sent you by
airgraph and which I will write out again if there's room, and a
song which I'll try and put in with this if I remember it. If you or
the publishers take violent exception to any of these and prepare
[sic] any of the others to be had from Blunden (or my mother may
have one or two) select for yourself. Of the 2 Soissons poems 1
appeared in the Cherwell, the other has never appeared anywhere. Villanelle of Spring Bells was in AUGURY, Time Eating has
never been published as far as I know (all these unpublished
Michael Meyer may have published since I left in the Cherwell or
grabbed for 8 Oxford Poets). The Marvel is unpublished, Kristin

was in Bolero, Poor Mary in Fords and Bridges of your editorship,
Stars in AUGURY, Canoe in The Cherwell, Francis Thompson in
Cherwell, Shadows in Cherwell, Burial of a God part 1 in King-
dom Come, the rest unpublished, Dotards do not think, un-
published, Russians in Kingdom Come, and the 2 from the
Middle East unpublished. You might include HAYDN — CLOCK
SYMPHONY (Kingdom Come). Now, as to commitments. Michael
Meyer has asked me for poems for a book called 8 Oxford Poets,
to be published by KEGAN PAUL, I believe, and with a foreword by
John Lehmann (or so he said). I gave him a free hand with my
stuff, as I couldn't do anything about it at the time. Sidney Keyes
of The Cherwell will know about this book (so perhaps will John
Lehmann) and what it involves, or whether it has died. If anything, supposing your project really and certainly materialized, I
would rather drop K.P. and Michael Meyer than you and Alan
and the Hogarth Press. But I would rather, of course, contribute
to both. Certainly I would rather you had better poems of mine
than K.P. if you quarrel over any. All this is somewhat unofficial
and not to be flung in the face of the progenitor of 8 Oxford POETS.
For your biographical note My full name is Keith Castellain
Douglas, my ancestry Scottish and pre-revolution French, I was
born in January (24th) 1920 and educated at Christ's Hospital
(shades of Blunden, Coleridge, Lamb, Leigh Hunt etc.) and of
course Merton Coll. Oxon where apart from Groups and Editorship of Cherwell I have no distinctions, but a year to go. I am
interested in clothes, drawing and painting (my own and other
people's), horses . . . music, ballet, stage design.* Recreations,
tap-dancing, rugger, water-polo, competitive swimming. That
should be more than enough. On the other side I'll try and put
poems. [He included copies of Song: 'Do I wonder away too far'
and 'Negative Information'.] Is this Michael Swan of whom you
speak an ex-schoolfellow of mine with a glass eye? If he is, he
dislikes me intensely, or did. But perhaps it's someone else, even
someone I should have heard of. By the way you understand I'm
not able to copy an [sic] MSS out so please try and return them.
* Present work — 2nd Lieut. Royal Armoured Corps.

[Keith Douglas]

[*?26 October 1941*]   *Notts SR Yeo MEF*

Dear Edmund, Here are 2 more poems, probably I think the last for some time, as my convalescent period which has consisted of doing nothing but sunbathe and bathe in the Mediterranean, is now over. I return to duty and the Notts. YEO. m.e.f. the day after tomorrow. I gather from rumours that duty even then is not over heavy and I may still get an occasional bathe. I've not yet paid my respects to Jerusalem which I suppose I ought to do before I leave this country. Those who have, however, seem little impressed. I have been for some very long walks along the shore and on although it's Palestinian winter it's hot enough in the day time — I consumed 4 ginger beers within two minutes of my return from my walk yesterday. I stick to ginger beer because the only available beer is Australian. The Mess is almost too luxurious and certainly too expensive. However in a day or two I shall once more live among sand, lizards, flies and mosquitoes, not forgetting the feverbringing diminutive sandfly. I have not had sandfly fever yet so I must have one or two 'goes' of it before I become immune I suppose. I hope to hear from you sometime. The Post Office, possibly even the army, will supply you with one of these or an Airgraph form.

    Love to Sylva   *Keith*

Adams

Walking alone beside the beach
where the Mediterranean turns in sleep
under the cliffs' demiarch,

walking thinking slowly I see
a dead bird & a live bird
the dead eyeless, but with a bright eye

the live bird discovered me
stepping from a black rock into the air:
leave the dead bird to lie. Watch him fly

electric, brilliant blue
beneath he is orange, like flame —
colours I can't believe are so;

as legendary flowers bloom
incendiary in tint, a focal point
like Adams in a room.

Adams is like a bird
alert (high on his pinnacle of air
he does not hear you, someone said);

in appearance he is bird-eyed,
the bones of his face are
like the hollow bones of a bird.

And he stood by the elegant wall
between two pictures hanging there
certain of homage from us all

as through the mind this minute
he draws the universe
and, like our admiration, dresses in it

towering like the cliffs of this coast
with his stilletto wing
and orange on his breast:

he sucked up, utterly drained
the colour of my sea,
the yellow of this tidal ground,

swallowing my thought
swallows all those dark fish there
that a rock hides from sunlight.

Till Rest, cries my mind to Adams' ghost;
only go elsewhere, let me alone
creep into the dead bird, cease to exist.

                                        Nathanya 1941

The 2 Virtues

Love me, and though you next experiment
with Arabian books, or search the exact centre
and the limit of love's continent
with an orator, a dancer, or a sailor
there's none so fierce as I nor so inconstant.

I've the two virtues of a lover
hot as the Indies, mutable as weather.

Hot, since of his own heat must
the lover touch you to a flame
firing the heart and its imprisoning dust
like saints, to be in heaven when they burn
reciprocating heat; alight remain
until the flames die out above
the dying salamander, love.

Then being true to love, I'll be inconstant;
not to be so, would cheat you of the last
and most of love, sorrow's violent
and rich effect. In that lagoon the lost,
the drowned heart is wonderfully recast
and made into a marvel by the sea,
that stone, that jewel tranquillity.

Sarafand 1941

Sorry about all these alterations — I copied from the wrong version. Hope it's intelligible.

J. C. HALL to MRS DOUGLAS (extract)
30 October 1941

If you have any more definite address [for Keith] perhaps you would let me know as I should like to write to him again soon. Apart from the project, it is stimulating and necessary for writers to keep in communication with each other and certainly Keith seemed one of the most promising poets I knew at Oxford — or since. His work is perhaps rather far removed from reality, but it has a perfection which is extraordinary among the poets of his generation (by the way, I speak as one of his age). . . .
P.S. If you have any recent poems of Keith's which show his reaction to the war, I should be most interested.

On 5 March Hall wrote again. The selection had been returned, perhaps because of the acute paper shortage. Alan Rook had found another publisher. Sending back to

Mrs Douglas copies of the poems he had, including the 'Song: Do I wander . . .', 'Negative Information' and 'These grasses . . .', he added: 'Frankly, I don't think any of these poems show Keith at his best, but I suppose circumstances are not very conducive to the writing of poetry!' Mrs Douglas took up his suggestion of sending them on to Blunden.

20 March 1942   *Merton College*

Dear Mrs Douglas, No, nothing had been heard lately from Keith and I am very glad you can give so merry an account of him in several of his familiar rôles (though I don't remember him slaying an Arab here.) So long as he escapes from the daughters of Zion in Cairo all may be well. I saw Jean Turner briefly a few days ago, at least it must have been her, she said she was, but she was in a blue uniform and hat rather like a piedish. Of N. Ilett [a school friend of Douglas] and Hamo Sassoon I have no word. But everyone suddenly turns up here and I hope the war will end while they are still doing it: sorry K.C.D. is too far off to do it. My critical faculties are worn out (today alone I have returned 3 large MS. works with opinions to their authors) and I can only say there's lots of life in the observation and intellectual curiosity of Keith's new pieces, but they are rather 'private' poetry and I wish he'd start up a good TUNE we could all catch. For there is plenty of commentary verse going round, but it's time someone got clear of it, and Keith could. This however may well be a cry from the tomb.

I'll send him a word with whatever Merton news there may be —

Best respects   Yours sincerely   *E. Blunden*

By March 1942 Douglas had joined and left the Sherwood Rangers Yeomanry, first being posted away on a camouflage course and then, temporarily, to a staff post.

1 March 1942   *HQ10 Armd Bde MEF*

Dear Edmund — Thank you very much for your letter — you

really must get hold of an airgraph form so that it takes a few months less to get here. I am incapable of being decently content I'm afraid. I was fed up with sitting in camp doing nothing. Now I am 10 times fedder up with being an elegant little staff officer with quite a lot to do, and no chance of getting back to the regiment. Mon général is one Clarke, who says you were his Intelligence Officer in the last show — 'Marvellous feller, always bringin' me reports in astonishin'ly neat handwritin', astonishin'ly neat. And then he'd dish in a bit of astonishin'ly good poetry, too. Well, you'd better write and tell him I'm still tickin' over, what? Good.' I am getting a certain amount of flying and going down to Cairo by plane tomorrow — my job is Camouflage, and the only comfort is that one day I may be sent up to the front line to observe, and I think if I do go General Clarke will find it an astonishin' long time before they find where the feller's got to — puttin' in a bit of fightin' on the sly, what? At the moment I am just getting used to living in a house and having a bath every night. I have a room distempered in light blue and unfurnished except for a wash stand sans basin and a very battered dresser (and my camp bed and basin). The dresser is somewhat brightened by a few Penguin covers, and I soon evolved a method of mural design by pencil and nail-file, which produces three tones, black pencil, blue wall about the colour of that [the letter paper], and white plaster where I scratch with the nail-file. So I have covered the walls with ballet dancers. Eventually I bought some paint and did a large group portraying Der Tod und das Mädchen, to my own choreography and without costumes except for death's cloak. Colours being black, blue and white, with a red backcloth behind painted like red clouds, and the words décor, choreography, mime set at angles round the design in this sort of lettering, [written in open-face] only somewhat neater and better-proportioned. I've had several letters from Jean Turner whom I think you know. She is now a Wren and likes it, except for the stiff collars. Stella Joan App. also writes occasionally — I hear Betty App. caught [eight words illegible]

I've heard no more of Eliot but I daresay I shall be able to catch up with him afterwards: I certainly seem to be in for cellophane preservation while the others do the dirty work and get all the experience I wanted.

I had an accident last time I was in Cairo and killed an Arab — he did the usual chicken-crossing-the road stunt, at the double, from behind a stationary vehicle. I was exonerated but somewhat shaken. It is curious how doll-like a broken up body looks, in spite of blood. A pity it's not so odourless as a doll.

I've been disappointed in attempts to meet anyone interesting in Palestine. The Jews resemble rabbits exactly except in gracefulness and pleasant appearance. The girls are lovely until they marry, which they seem to do about 16, and from then on are dirty, slovenly, smelly, sullen, and permanently (it appears) in the last and most ungainly stages of pregnancy. The men seldom wash or shave and are usually out of condition and wear sort of prismatic spectacles. They are also sullen unless behind a counter, a bar, or a tray. And yet there must be many of the brilliant refugees hidden among these morons. Perhaps I'll find them yet. With love to Sylva   *Keith*

29 March 1942   *Merton College*

My dear Keith, Your letter owning up to the fate of the Arab has just come, but your Mother had reported that troublesome accident, and sent some of your later poems. These were good Douglas poems, and all I want is some poems from you on external themes, especially from the land of Ozymandias. Otherwise a collection of your verse will scarcely show variety enough for your powers. But as I told your Mother whatever I say on literature at present is quite hopeless, for I am tired out as a critic by requests to read MSS. of all sorts, or it may be printed vols. Even now there are many Authors in the land who think of any Author already in progress and send him large parcels of their work (all sorts — from philosophic reviews of chivalric tradition to fantasies about bombing raids.) I am also almost at the end of my giving talks to Societies, chairing literary discussions and so on, except what Oxford really has to have.

But, something more important: My warmest congratulations to you on your being attached to the headquarters of Genl. J. G. W. Clark. With him in mind I lately wrote an article appearing in the *T.L.S.*, and now you are serving under him! I wish I was. But he sleepeth not, and his young men have to be rather superhuman. He may tell you some pleasant anecdotes of Genl. M. L. Hornby if you persuade him. He plays golf I believe better than most men. His appalling superiority to any kind of fear was not lost upon me. I last saw him near Gouzeaucourt, indeed walked the trenches with him by Gauche Wood, and he was looking extremely comfortable with the German offensive about to burst upon us. Please offer him my devoted Respects (and apologies for many shortcomings in 1917–1918, which I should try to overcome now with what little wisdom has come since.) My advice is, stick to Gen¹. Clark. (I am sure he will enjoy your display of the Fine Arts applied to your billet, for he always had an aesthetic sense, even about the conduct of a raid.)

Not long ago we had a glimpse of Jean Turner, nice modest sensible girl, looking efficient in her uniform; she spoke of a kind of place to place duty of a Bureaucratic tinge. Appletonian visits occur, but whether the schemes of Father A. come to anything the news doesn't show. There was one for dispensing Poetry to the troops, but the idea is scarcely new, and the troops are equal to emergencies. G. Townend is with us as yet, and R. Green comes for his meadow round every Wednesday.

A friend arrives with a book of biographical interest: the subject 'by the time he was 14 had forgotten his Sanskrit'. So you may have forgotten your Old Norse. There are those in Oxford who do not.

Took a walk in Magdalen grounds yesterday, where the crocus and a starry blue flower which I cannot name were doing well in spite of a sharp East wind, today the sun is stronger and maybe the green will soon look like April's proper hue. We have done with one more Term, but the vacation seems to be as elusive as ever. The *Mitre* has taken to closing on Sunday mornings, not that this will inconvenience you just at present; perhaps the Cairo branch will be working. I have seen no eminent Artists to tell you about, except Albert Rutherston who was eloquent on the disadvantages of the painter compared with the writer — not the cash side so much as that of really keeping one's subject in view at the right time. I think this must mean that one of his models escaped from the Ashmolean at speed. But he was a charming talker on this ancient theme of the difference between the arts. I fear you won't have much time to study it just now, but look forward to the period when you will.

Sylva reverbs best wishes, and I — Yours ever   *E. Blunden*

In May Hall found a new publisher for the selection, with Norman Nicholson replacing Alan Rook. In August Hall signed the contract with John Bale & Staples for the book which was to be No 3 in their series 'The Modern Reading

Library'. Douglas would be represented by about sixteen poems and each of the poets would receive a royalty of one penny per copy. In the Middle East Douglas's poems started to appear in *Citadel*, edited by David Hicks who shared a flat with Bernard Spencer, where Douglas stayed when in Cairo. In March 1943 *Citadel* printed a piece in which Douglas returned to a subject which had interested him at school and Oxford. Hicks may well have asked for it as a space-filler: the lack of substance is impressive enough to be calculated.

❧

The Butterflies

From time to time you may still see in the booksellers' windows one or two of these volumes, still glaring in colour, a garish and perfectly characteristic brilliance, on whose jackets writhe the sinister convolutions of Aubrey Beardsley's pen. Someone as lucky as those who looked two years ago into Basil Blackwell's window in Broad Street, Oxford may come upon a full set of them. Like rare butterflies, they may sometimes be found asleep on secluded shelves; and it is not as an affectation that I call them butterflies, for their whole character is fritillary or mothlike, their contents, even their contributors, of a butterfly nature. Look into any of Beardsley's or Walter Crane's whorling cover designs, and you will see as likely as not the butterfly crouching there; beside the words in a hideous kind of enlarged typescript:

THE YELLOW BOOK

Is it as a confession of having no idea for a title that this apparently redundant trio of words announces the book's identity — as a collection of verse lines is uncompromisingly headed **poem**? There is more to it. Yellow, whatever its significance for readers of wild west meant to the sponsors of the Yellow Book the quality of decadence, of brilliance, the flag of the Hedonist and the Happy Hypocrite. To announce therefore this yellow volume as yellow, is in effect to say: 'Yes, it's yellow. Consider the significance of that, before you open it.' An injunction I shall obey.

I have no books of reference and no convenient quotations, to restate what has been said, particularly by writers on the end of the XIXth Century about la Fin de Siècle and its implications. As some pretend to notice an uncanny silence imposing itself on all conversations at twenty minutes before and after the hour, students of Literature, History and Art have claimed that at these moments, the end of centuries, there is an exactly contrary phenomenon, a blaze of noise, a shout of colour, as though Time had gone one better than Vespasian and cried: 'A Century should die dancing'. I am not inclined to examine the obsequies of previous centuries to give credence to this theory. It has been done and anyone can do it again, whom the occupation amuses. But in the last years of the XIXth Century there is plenty of shouting and dancing — some the simplest and emptiest Ta-ra-ra-boomdiay (this song has already been rightly noted an anthem of the times) — some the briliant utterances, the madder music and stronger wine, inflaming the world to create a million lunatic structures of absolute perfection, until — for God's sake, what else can end it — the whole explodes, or is burnt out.

Open one of these cloth-bound books: perhaps an old ribbon or a letter in spidery script will fall out from between two of the pages and you may guess, but never know, what piece it marked among these dying effusions, or why. Look at the signature: perhaps it is one of those florid names you will discover in the list of contributors — Oscar O'Flaherty Wills Wylde,[1] Frederick Baron Corvo, Aubrey Beardsley, Ernest Christopher Dowson, Max Beerbohm, Henry Harland, and who can recollect how many obscure, whom either the fire consumed as it consumed with hellish ferocity Wylde, Corvo, Beardsley, Dowson or who managed like Beerbohm and Harland, to escape perhaps because they stood further away.

To come upon the literary or biographical remains of these men, anywhere in the world — and they appear at unexpected moments — is always to feel a little of the fire under your hand yet. I once went to a party in Wylde's old room in Magdalen: it is a large and undistinguished room now, with the usual flaccid college furniture and a marble fireplace. On the big window facing Magdalen Bridge are Wylde's five initial letters, scratched on the glass with a diamond: beside them is a bullet hole, and the bullet which made it has chipped away some of the horrible fireplace. In this room I remember nothing else, except the figure of a large, quite corpulent man, with the smallest mouth I ever saw picked out in mauve lipstick against his moonlike cheeks. He discussed church music in a sibilant precise voice. Who fired the bullet, and at whom, whether at Wylde or at one of his successors, no one has ever told me: whoever it was stood after dark on

Magdalen Bridge to fire at a figure inside a lighted room. I am perhaps wrong to imagine it was anything but my own suscep- tibilities which touched me with the sensation of assisting at some kind of diabolism, as I stood by the damaged fireplace and listened to the soft voice discoursing on Walmisley in B Minor.

Religion, not conservative Protestantism, but Catholicism which loves beauty and ritual and fills the upper air with semi- divine saints and devils, is often part of the inspiration of these writers. Frederick Baron Corvo, that bogus nobleman and literary alchymist, was not the only one of them whose ambition it was to take Orders. Gerard Manley Hopkins is a more obvious example of Roman Catholic 'yellow' writer, who abandons himself only to the possibilities of words. But Corvo, Frederick Rolfe, (which he wrote finally Fr. Rolfe, for Frederick, and as he wished it could have been, father), was frustrated in his aim. This paranoiac spiteful homosexual genius, whom the Scots College in Rome expelled, reasonably, as unsuitable for priesthood, and who died a procurer of beautiful boys in Venice, in extreme poverty and misery; wrote to comfort himself his life from the palm of his left hand, his potential life. It was, it is, a masterpiece: the story of the rejected candidate for priesthood, George Arthur Rose, who became Pope Hadrian VII. In this dream life he did not posture, but went from strength to strength without hesitation, as great as Innocent but holier. Even in fiction however his enemies pursued him. He was assassinated in Rome, upon an ornamental and ominous day . . .

> How bright the sunlight was, on the warm grey stones, on the ripe Roman skins, on vermilion and lavender and blue and gold, on the indecent grotesque blackness of two blotches, on Apostolic whiteness and the rose of blood.

Upon all the colours of the butterfly, who skims across these pictures picking and sipping at the brightest plants. In Beardsley's he often alights; in whose black and white creations lay effects of most violent colour; as in his white face with that amazing nose, a strange narrow prow or promontory of bone, the ominous impending hair from beneath which the eyes glitter, is enough dangerous colour and flame to attract the eye of insects and men. Those ladies in a maze of their own tresses and draperies, those marble statues, fauns, and voluted grasses, were the creatures of a brain burning down, destroyed by flames of inspiration as the body burned with the ravages of consumption.

Ernest Christopher Dowson is now known almost solely for that often-quotable verse Cynara: he showed an inclination towards beautiful designs in verse comparable with Beardsley's penwork, in villanelles and other repetitive verses, melancholy and romantic, but seldom sickly, saved by a restraining cynicism. 'A little passionately, not at all,' he burnt, he flickered, at times he was even calm. Dowson is the connecting link (Symons also) with Verlaine; and it may be the best way to explain the whole contents and nature of the Yellow Book, which contains translations of Verlaine and Baudelaire, to remark that these English writers, although more politely attired, were treading a path parallel with Baudelaire, Verlaine, Rimbaud in France. The difference between these ornate and, it must be admitted, occasionally redundant patterns of Beardsley, Dowson and Corvo, and the sordid stark or detailed utter bathing in evil, the 'Surrealism in Morals' of Baudelaire is not as great a difference as it may seem. Evil is never far from the hectic beauty of the Yellow Book's creators: Oscar Wylde's Salome, even the Picture of Dorian Gray, point what I mean.

The Yellow Book is not entirely a feast of evil — its list of contributors includes the innocent name of Kenneth Grahame, and at least one of its artists remained until his death a few years ago a contributor to that pillar of unhumorous respectability — as it then was — **Punch**.

Even the 'Stories Toto told me' of Fr. Rolfe are not more sinister than Harland's own sweet but witty nothings. It was in the Yellow Book that Max Beerbohm's Happy Hypocrite first appeared, which, involved and exquisite though it is as any of the evilly beautiful pieces, is nothing but a charming fairy tale with a simple and quite moral moral. Though as an artist probably the greatest of them — he writes effortlessly where others cannot disguise their labour — and though he created the heartless Zuleika Dobson, who slew with her beauty all the male undergraduate members of the University of Oxford before instructing her maid to purchase tickets for Cambridge; Beerbohm is a benevolent ornamenter, not touched or enamoured of evil. So he escaped with his life, escaped entirely.

I wish I had even one copy of the Yellow Book before me, or the space to put down a few more of the disjointed lines I can still evoke to quote. But these haphazard references, and this note in spite of its obvious failure to explore several avenues, may be enough to draw the attention of some who might have missed it, to this strange book, surely the only periodical[2] — it was a quarterly — to have embalmed, in its comparatively few numbers the essential body of the English literature of a short, tremendously important epoch, and the literary remains of many strange souls who still await their biographers.

1   The names are deleted by KD in his copy, with the note: 'curiously enough Wylde never wrote anything for the Y.B.'
2   KD noted on his copy: 'What about *The Savoy*?'

The same issue of *Citadel* included a poem by Douglas which the reader must have found hard to connect with the author of 'The Butterflies'. The poem, 'Dead Men', vividly portrayed the desert battlefield. At the end of October 1942 Douglas had put into effect the scheme he had announced to Blunden the previous March. He had disobeyed orders, left his staff post and rejoined his regiment. He had not done so earlier, perhaps, because of a relationship with Milena Guttierez-Pegna in Alexandria. That relationship ended suddenly at the start of October. He did so now, because of the build up and commencement of the battle of El Alamein.

To JOHN HALL
postmark: 29 October 1942   *Cairo*

The Knife

Can I explain this to you? Your eyes
are entrances the mouths of caves
I issue from wonderful interiors
upon a blessed sea and a fine day
from inside these caves I look and dream.

Your hair explicable as a waterfall
in some black liquid cooled by legend
fell across my thought in a moment
became a garment I am naked without
lines drawn across through morning and evening.

And in your body each minute I died
moving your thigh could disinter me
from a grave in a distant city:
your breasts deserted by cloth, clothed in twilight
filled me with tears, sweet cups of flesh.

Yes, to touch two fingers made us worlds
stars, waters, promontories, chaos,
swooning in elements without form or time
come down through long seas among sea marvels
embracing like survivors on our islands.

This I think happened to us together
though now no shadow of it flickers in your hands
your eyes look down the banal streets
if I talk to you I might be a bird
with a message, a dead man, a photograph.

For M. G-P

The Offensive

I

Tonight's a moonlit cup
and holds the liquid time
that will run out in flame
in poison we shall sup.

The moon's at home in a passion
of foreboding. Her lord
the martial sun, abroad
this month will see Time fashion

the action we begin
and Time will cage again
the devils we let run
whether we lose or win:

in the month's dregs will
a month hence, some descry

the too late prophecy
of what the month lets fall.

This overture of quiet
is a minute to think on
the quiet like a curtain
when the piece is complete.

So in conjecture stands
my starlit body; the mind
mobile as a fox sneaks round
the sleepers waiting for their wounds.

This overture of quiet
is a minute to think on
the quiet like a curtain
when the piece is complete.

II

The stars dead heroes in the sky
may well approve the way you die
nor will the sun
revile those who survive because
for the dying and promising there was
these evils remain:

when you are dead and the harm done
the orators and clerks go on
the rulers of interims and wars
effete and stable as stars.

The stars in their fragile house
are the heavenly symbols of a class
dead in their seats;
the officious sun goes round
organising life, and what he's planned
Time comes and eats.

The sun goes round and the stars go round
the nature of eternity is circular
and man must spend a life to find
all our successes and failures are similar.

If you don't want any of these, please send them on to my
mother, c/o National Provincial Bank Ltd. Staines, Middx., or
any better address you know.   *Keith Douglas*

[*Fragment on the first page of an Italian exercise book, 'Qaderno',
taken from the desert battlefield (May 1943)*]

To find myself on the eve of battle relegated to the congregation
of supply vehicles, fifty miles behind all the great events, seemed
to me at that time the most dishonourable fate that could have
overtaken me. Even as a camouflage officer, and after eight
months experience of the idiocy of departments, in sanguine
moods I had still hoped to triumph over them all and compel
some respect for my work, perhaps after I had lost respect for it
myself. Believing in the futility of introducing any scheme of
camouflage at this 11th hour, [. . .]

Abandoned draft, revising part of *Alamein to Zem Zem*
(unfinished; September 1943)

[. . .] the track were of a more combatant kind; infantry resting,
heavy and medium gunners and the usual light anti-aircraft. A
few staff and liaison officers in jeeps and staff cars still passed.
The smaller cars were often identifiable only by their passengers'
heads showing out of enveloping dustclouds. But the traffic was
now mostly of supply lorries moving between their fighting men
and their supply of 'B' echelons.

Fifteen miles from our starting point and about four miles in
rear of the regiment I found our own supply lorries in charge of
two officers whom I knew; Scotty, an ex NCO of the Scots Greys,
now a captain, and Roger, a gawky young Major whom no one
would have suspected of being an old Etonian. It was hard to
imagine him at a public school at all: he might have sprung,
miraculously enlarged but otherwise unaltered from an inky
bench in a preparatory school. No one would have been surprised
to find white mice in Roger's pockets. On these two I had to test
my story. Being a little afraid they would laugh at the idea of my
running back to the regiment and destroy my faith in my own
plans, I began by greeting them and asking where the regiment
was. 'A few miles up the road' Scotty said. 'They're out of action

at the moment but they're expecting to go in again any time. Have you come back?' I said that depended on whether the Colonel thought I would be any use to him. 'Oh he'll be glad to see *you* I don't think "A" Squadron's got many officers left' said Scotty. 'We'd a bad day the other day. I lost all my stuff the same night. One of the petrol lorries got hit when we were going through a minefield. It lit up the whole place and they just threw over everything they had.' This was the sort of thing one had heard many times, but this time it meant something to me. I didn't ask who had been killed or wounded for the moment but said goodbye to them and pushed on up the track to join the regiment. I was encouraged by Scotty's saying I should be needed.

We found the tanks and trucks of the regiment scattered about some way off the track, not much dispersed; the men were 'doing maintenance'. A tall Ordnance Officer whom I had never seen before directed me to the same fifteen hundredweight truck which had been the Orderly Room in the training area at Wadi Natrun. In some apprehension I walked across between the tanks to this truck for the final and decisive interview. I looked about among the men as I went, but saw only one or two familiar faces. The personnel of the regiment alters surprisingly, even in a few months. I looked about for Stanley, my squadron leader and for Sam and Johnny who had been troop leaders with me but I could not see any of them. The Colonel, beautifully dressed, and with his habitual indolence of hand, returned my salute from inside the fifteen hundredweight.

He was sitting with Derek, the Adjutant, a boy with red hair and a girl's face, one of the original members of the regiment and one of our half dozen Old Etonians. The Colonel's nickname was Flash, which in one word said what many could not better. He was a dandy, superficially forceful, outwardly effeminate and inwardly having a woman's illogical and impulsive processes of mind; unjust and unskilled; gallant, occasionally brilliant: a careerist, gambler and member of Parliament. I saluted and said to him: — 'Good evening Sir. I've escaped from Division for the moment, and I wondered if I should be any use to you here.' 'Well Keith,' stroking his moustache, looking like a contented ginger cat, 'We're *most* glad to see you, er, as always. All the officers in "A" Squadron except Andrew are casualties, so I'm sure he'll welcome you with open arms. We shall be going into action again either tonight or tomorrow morning, so you'd better go and, er, take over a troop now.' Derek, his mind on returns and casualty states, asked if I were definitely posted back to the regiment, and I had to explain my escape. 'Well done,' said Flash. 'I think a policy of Masterly Inactivity is indicated. We'll take care of that.' As I walked away, there was no voice but that of my mind to say: 'Well, you asked for it; and you've got a bit more than you expected.' I could not help smiling; and the tremendous question was decided, so suddenly and definitely after eight months. Palestine had receded in a moment to the other side of the world, and a few miles to the west, where the sounds of gunfire had intensified, lay the German armies. There lay also so many strange scenes, the answers to so many questions.

Andrew I found sitting beside his tank. I had met him before but when he looked up at my approach I saw he did not recognise me. He was not young, and although at the moment an acting major about to go into action in a tank for the first time in his life, Andrew had already seen service in Abyssinia, where he had organised the patriots, those local levies who were with difficulty and much gold persuaded to fight against the Italians. From Abyssinia he had come to Cairo as a Colonel in some sort of Intelligence job at GHQ. And from there, suddenly smitten with a nostalgia for the regiment, he had returned to it, foregoing his job and his rank of Colonel, as a captain. What happened after that is an argument against such spectacular conduct. It was not a success; he found the regiment changed out of all recognition, and could never get used to the new ways and faces: nor did he ever learn his new job. But this we had yet to find out. For the moment we were all impressed by his courage and fine disregard of material honours, and I was as much his admirer as anyone.

He was a small man with yellowish hair turning grey, sitting on a petrol tin and marking the cellophane surface of his mapcase with a coloured chinagraph pencil. His face was brick-red with sun and wind, the skin cracking on his lips and nose. He wore a grey flannel shirt, a pair of old yellow corduroy trousers and sandals over army socks. Round his mahogany coloured neck a blue silk handkerchief was twisted and tied like a stock, and on his head was a beret. Like most ex-cavalrymen he had no idea how to wear it. I reported to him, resplendent if a little dusty in my polished cap and belt. He allotted me two tanks there not being enough on the squadron strength to make sub-units of more than two. I drove the two tonner with my kit on it, to one of these tanks and began to unload and sort out my belongings. Ward and I laid them, together with the three bags of rations which we had brought away from the superabundant stores of them at Division, in a pattern on the sand. The corporal whom I had relieved as tank commander staggered off under an unwieldy bundle of bedding and kit, insecurely confined by a groundsheet.

Ward was to go for the duration of the battle to the technical stores lorry, where he had a friend and where he could make himself useful. To him I handed over the greater part of my belongings — the style in which I had travelled at Divisional headquarters being now outmoded. I kept a halfshare of the three bags of rations which I distributed between the two tank crews; this amounting to several tins of bully beef, of course; one or two of first American white potatoes; and some greater treasures, tins of American bacon rashers, and of fruit and condensed milk. A pair of clean socks were filled, one with tea, the other with sugar. I changed my peaked cap for a beret, and retained a small cricket bag with shirts, slacks, washing and shaving kit, writing paper, a camera, and a Penguin Shakespeare's Sonnets. Rolled up in my valise and bedding were a suit of battle dress, my revolver with six rounds in it, and a British Warm. In my pocket, instead of my First Field Dressing, which I had lost, I put a hunting flask of Scotch Whisky; and in the locker on the side of the tank in addition to the rations I put some tins of NAAFI coffee and OXO cubes bought in Alexandria. I felt the satisfaction of anyone beginning an expedition in contemplating my assembled stores and in bestowing them.

As soon as this was finished I began to make the acquaintance of the tank crews. My own tank was a Mark Three Crusader, then comparatively new to us all. I had once been inside the Mark Two, which had a two pounder gun and a four man crew, and was now superseded by this tank with a six pounder and only three in the crew; the place of the fourth being taken up by the breech mechanism of the six pounder. This tank is the best-looking tank I ever saw, whatever its shortcoming of performance. It is lowbuilt, which in desert warfare and indeed in all tank warfare is a first consideration. This gives it together with its lines and its smooth suspension on five great wheels a side, the appearance almost of a speedboat. To see these tanks crossing country at speed was a thrill which seemed inexhaustible, equal with that of riding in them; many times it encouraged us. And although we often cursed them on the whole we were proud of them.

From underneath this particular tank a pair of boots protruded. As I looked at them, my mind being still by a matter of two days untrained to it, the inevitable association of ideas did not take place. The whole man emerged, muttering in a Glaswegian monotone. He was a small chap with a disgruntled urchin's face, called Mudie. I found him, during the weeks I spent with him, to be lazy, dirty, (this was incidental and applied to us all), permanently discontented and a most amusing talker. In battle he did not have much opportunity, and was silent even during rests and meals; but at all other times he would wake up talking, as birds do, at the first gleam of light, long before dawn; and he would still be talking, in his invariable monotone, long after dark. He was the driver of the tank. Mudie was a reservist and so was the gunner, Evan, who looked and was a much harder case than Mudie. Evan hardly spoke at all, but if drawn into conversation would reveal — if he were talking to an officer — a number of injustices under which he was suffering at the moment, introducing them with a calculated air of weariness and 'it doesn't matter now' as though he had been so worn down by the callousness of his superiors as to entertain no more hope of redress. In conversation with his fellows — I say fellows because I don't think he had or wanted any friends — he affected a kind of snarling wit; and he never did anything that was not in the end for his own profit, save on one occasion. Mudie would often do things for other people, but Evan would help no one but an officer, and then only if he could not well avoid it. Yet twice he was unexpectedly quick and efficient, as I shall describe.

We were at an hour's notice to move. This meant not that we should move in an hour's time, but that if we did move we should have an hour in which to prepare for it. When I had sorted out my belongings and eaten some meat and vegetable stew washed down with coffee, I lay down on my bedding with a magazine which someone had left on the tank. I glanced only vaguely at the pages, thinking over the changes of the last few days, and confronting myself with the future. Desultory thumps sounded in the distance and occasionally large bushes of dust sprang up on the skyline, or a plane droned across very high up in the unvarying blue air. Men passed and repassed, shouting to each other, laughing, singing and whistling the same incomplete, ironical phrases from dance tunes as they always did. Metallic

sounds merged with hum of light and heavy engines at a distance. Occasionally a machine gun would sputter for a few
seconds as it was tested or cleared. The whole pot-pourri of
sounds mixing in the heat of declining afternoon would have put
me to sleep, but for my own excitement and apprehensions, and
the indefatigable flies.

I was not dissatisfied. I still felt the exhilaration of cutting
myself free from the whole net of inefficiency and departmental
bullshit that had seemed to have me quite caught up in Divisional
Headquarters. I had exchanged a vague and general existence for
a particular and perhaps a short one. And I had never realised how
ashamed of myself I had been in my safe staff job, until with my
escape this feeling was suddenly gone. I had in my mind that
feeling of almost unstable lightness which is felt physically
immediately after putting down a very heavy weight. All my
awkward mental arguments and enquiries about the future were
shelved, perhaps permanently. I got out my writing paper and
wrote two letters, one to my mother and one to David Hicks in
Cairo. Although in writing these letters, (which of course got lost
and were never posted) I felt very dramatic, the tone of them was
not particularly theatrical. To my mother I wrote that I rejoiced to
have escaped at long last from Division, and be back with the
regiment. I sent to Hicks a poem which I had written during my
last days at Div. HQ based on the idea of the ominous pregnancy
of the moon which at the beginning of the battle was in its first
quarter. I asked him to see that this poem got home as I had not
got a stamp or an airgraph, and said he could print it in the British
Council magazine Citadel if he liked. This he subsequently did
when I sent him the poem from hospital.

I had asked Andrew one or two general questions about training
in the hope of not showing myself too ignorant in my first action,
but it was fairly plain that he knew no more himself than I did. 'I
shouldn't worry, old boy,' was all he would say. 'The squadron
and troop leaders don't use maps much and there are no codes at
all. Just talk as you like over the air — except for map references of
course — but you won't need those. You'll find it quite simple.'
When I had written my letters I got into the turret with Evan and
tried to learn its geography. My place as tank commander was on
the right of the six pounder. I had a seat from which I could look
out through a periscope. This afforded a very small view, and in
action all tank commanders stand on the floors of their turrets so
that their eyes are clear of the top, or actually sit in the manhole of

the turret with their legs dangling inside. Behind the breech of the six pounder is a metal shield to protect the crew against the recoil of the gun which leaps back about a foot when it is fired. On my side of the six pounder was a rack for a box of machine gun ammunition the belt of which had to run over the top of the six pounder and into the feed slide of the BESA machine gun mounted on the other side of it. There were also two smoke dischargers to be operated by me. Stacked round the sides of the turret were the six pounder shells, nose downwards; hand grenades, smoke grenades, and boxes of machine gun ammunition. At the back of the turret, on a shelf, stood the wireless set with its control boxes for switching from the 'A' set to internal communication between the crew, and on top of the wireless set a pair of binoculars, wireless spare parts and tommy gun magazines. There was a Tommy gun in a clip on Evan's side of the turret. Stencilled all over the turret with infinite and wasted care were hundreds of redundant little labels — WIRELESS SPARES . . . GRENADES . . . BINOCULARS . . . 6PDR . . . etc. We used sometimes to amuse ourselves by working out how much paint and time were wasted in putting on these labels, since even the people who loaded the tanks must have known where the things went after they had loaded the first ten or so, and we certainly had no time or need to be looking at labels. When we were in action there were also Penguin books, chocolate or boiled sweets when we could get them, biscuits, a tin of processed cheese, and a knife stowed on the shelf at the back of the turret. We were lucky enough to begin the battle with a tin of Australian butter as well.

About dusk the wireless in all tanks were switched on and netted to the regimental control station, to make sure everyone's set was as far as possible on the same frequency. Each station, like 2LO in early broadcasting, was known by a call sign, by which it announced itself and was called up by control stations. Before dark I went across to see that my other tank was ready to move, completely filled with rations, kit, petrol, oil, ammunition and water. I stayed some time talking to the crew. The corporal, Trueman, had already been captured and recaptured during the first four days of the battle. He said the Germans had treated him very well, and seemed quite cheerful — so did his gunner and driver — at the prospect of going into action again. This was more than could be said of Evan and Mudie who grew dourer and more taciturn every minute.

I lay down to sleep in my clothes covered with my British Warm and blankets, for the nights were already beginning to be cold. Perhaps betrayed into a mood of more solemnity by the stars which were as clear as jewels on black velvet tonight, I suddenly found myself assuming that I was going to die tomorrow. For about a quarter of an hour, I considered to what possibilities of suffering, more than of death, I had laid myself open. This with the dramatic and emotional part of me. But my senses of proportion and humour like two court jesters, humorously quoting to me Bishop Ken's hymn, 'Live each day as if 'twere thy last', had soon chased away the tragic poet, and I drifted away on a tide of odd thoughts watching the various signs of battle in the lower sky. I believe I persuaded myself that I had passed the worst ordeals of anticipatory fear, and that there would be not time for sharp and instantaneous fear in the busyness of battle. If I thought so I was not long to remain undeceived. The moon now grown much greater than when she had inspired my poem, presided over a variety of lesser lights: starshells, traces of orange, green red, and a harsh white and the deeper colours of explosions. We were still at an hour's notice.

Someone shook me out of my sleep at the cold hour of four o'clock. Somewhat to my surprise I woke immediately to the full consciousness of where I was. For I had feared as I dropped asleep, that the morning might surprise me at my least heroic hour. The moment I was wakeful I had to be busy. We were to move at five: before that engines had to be warmed up, orders to be given throughout the whole hierarchy from the Colonel to the tank crews. In the halflight the tanks seemed to crouch, cold-bloodedly alive, like toads. I touched the chilly metal shell of mine, my fingers amazed for a moment at its absolute hardness, and swung myself into the turret to get out my mapcase. Of course it had fallen down on the small circular floor of the turret. In getting down after it I contrived to hit my head on the base of the six pounder and scratch open both my hands: inside the turret there is less room even than in an aircraft, and it requires experience to move about. By the time I came up a general activity had begun to warm the appearance of the leaguer if not the air of it. The tanks were now half-hidden in clouds of blue smoke as their engines began one after another to grumble and the stagnant oil burnt away. This scene, with the silhouettes of men and turrets interrupted by curtains of smoke and the sky lightening behind them, was to be made familiar to me by many repetitions. Out of each turret like the voices of dwarfs, thin and cracked and bodyless, the voices of the operators and of the control set come. They speak to the usual accompaniment of 'mush', morse, odd squeals, and the peculiar jangling, like a barrel-organ, of an enemy jamming station.

———————————

Probably as a result of the vacillation of Brigade or of some even higher authority, nobody moved before seven o'clock, when the Crusader squadron — my squadron — moved out of the area and onto the other side of a track running north to south. Here we halted, having left the heavy squadrons of Shermans and Grants still scattered in leaguer, and were allowed to brew up. The immense moral satisfaction and recreation of brewing up was something I had never realised so clearly before. As soon as permission is given, all crews except those detailed for lookout duty swarm out of their turrets. The long boxes on the side of the tank are opened: tins of bacon or meat and vegetable, according to the time of day, are got out, while someone is lighting a fire on a petrol tin filled with a stiff paste of sand and petrol. A veteran blackened half of a petrol tin is unhooked from some extremity of the tank and filled with water for tea. Within five minutes a good crew has a cup of immensely strong and sweet hot tea to each man and sandwiches, for instance, of oatmeal biscuits fried in bacon fat and enclosing crisp bacon. If there is a little more time, it will probably be used to make another brew of tea from the same leaves, and to eat more biscuits spread with oleomargarine, — a horrible but wholesome synthetic — and Palestinian marmalade. This morning I found printed on my marmalade tin the name of the communal settlement at Givat Brenner; I had spent a day in being shown over it four or five months before. Thoughts of that fertile place and peaceful industrious community induced a minute or two of nostalgia and a less logical but more comforting sense of friends following me into this strange country. Soon after we had finished eating we were turned round and returned to camp. I never discovered why we made this picnic excursion. We did not move again until late afternoon when the regiment moved out, Crusaders leading, in single file onto the track up which I had come the day before. The head of the column turned westwards, only turrets and pennants, flown on the six foot aerials, showing above the billowing dust. I took a photograph of the column behind and in front of me.

That afternoon was still and sunny, the upper air clear, the ground churned everywhere into white dust by the endless traffic. The white dust lay very thickly rutted on the ground and mixed with the atmosphere like a mist for a foot or two above the desert. Even without looking at the formations lying beside the track it was possible to sense subdued activity on a huge scale everywhere. On the track, beside our own column of tanks moving up slowly screened and enveloped in their own dust, tanks and armoured cars passed us going out of battle and a renewed traffic of staff cars and jeeps made it clear that the front line had advanced since the previous night when few of them had been coming so far forward. These smaller vehicles bucketed in and out among the main streams of traffic. Up above in the clear sky a solitary aeroplane moved, bright silver in the sunlight, a pale line of exhaust marking its unhurried course. The Bofors gunners on either side of the track were running to their guns and soon opened a rapid thumping fire, like a titanic workman hammering. The silver body of the plane was surrounded by hundreds of little grey smudges, through which it sailed on serenely. From it there fell away, slowly and gracefully, an isolated shower of rain, a succession of glittering drops. I watched them descend a hundred feet before it occurred to me to consider their significance as well as their beauty. The column of tanks trundled forward, but the heads of their crews no longer showed. I dropped down in the turret and shouted to Evan, who was dozing in the gunner's seat: 'Someone's dropping some stuff.' He shouted back a question and adjusted his earphones. 'Bombs' I shouted into the microphone. Their noisy arrival somewhere on our right confirmed the word. Control called us over the air: 'Nuts one, is everybody O.K.?' '2 OK off' 'Three OK off' 'Four OK off' said the voices in my earphones. I completed the group: 'Five OK off.' The journey continued.

The view from a moving tank is that in a camera obscura or a silent film — in that since the engine drowns all other noises except explosions, the whole world moves silently. Men shout, lorries move, aircraft fly over, and all soundlessly; the noise of the tank being continuous, often for hours, ceases to be noticeable. I think it may have been this fact, that for so much of the time I saw everything without hearing the attendant noises, that led me to think of this country we were now entering on as an illimitable strange land, quite unrelated to real life, and made still stranger by its distorted scenery. Silence is a strange thing to us who are alive. We desire it, fear, worship, and hate it. If cats were worshipped, it was surely for their silence; swans are majestic and legendary creatures because of their silence and silent movements. And Stephen Crane speaks of a dead man on a battlefield who had the air of knowing the answer to life. It is the silence of the dead that gives them this air; their triumphant silence, proof against any questioner in the world.

A party of prisoners now appeared marching on our left. They were evidently very tired but looked about them with a good deal of interest, particularly at our column. I thought of the publicity photographs of glowering SS men in their tanks and glared at them through my goggles in the hope of looking like part of an inexorable War Machine myself. They must have been as much impressed with the strength and concentration of our forces by the time they reached their cage at the rear, as I was after coming through it all on my way to the front. About two hundred of them passed us, in batches, as we continued our journey. We looked at them with an interest equal to their own. They did not look very fearsome; they were almost all Germans with shapeless green or khaki drill uniforms and floppy peaked caps having a red white and black bullseye on them. The desert on either side of the track became more sparsely populated with vehicles and at length there were none but derelicts. The column halted at last so that my tank stood beside the burnt out wreck of a German Mark 4 Special, with its long gun and row of little wheels. Most of one side of it had been torn out, probably by the explosion of its own ammunition. Some charred clothing lay beside it, but there was no equipment, and no sign of the crew. The whole thing made a disconcerting cautionary picture. On the horizon to our front we could see two vehicles burning fiercely, from which expanding columns of black smoke slanted across the orange sky. We could see shells, visible by their traces as red yellow or white lights, sailing in apparently slow curves; they were being fired by tanks on our left, but were landing in dead ground to us. But now the light was ebbing perceptibly, and soon the burning vehicles and the shelltraces shone against the darkening sky. Enemy shells could be seen flying from beyond the ridge ahead of us. We were now spectators of the closing stages of the day's battle.

I dismounted and went to find Andrew, leaving Evan and Mudie silently examining the derelict tank: apparently we were to leaguer for the night nearby, and Andrew went away into the growing obscurity to receive his orders from the Colonel. He told me to prevent the tanks from wandering away and getting lost until he came back. But in the end he sent the Welsh sergeant,

Harding, to summon us back to him, and himself led us slowly, watching each the red rear light of the tank in front of him, into our position for the night. The Crusaders were drawn up in two rows in front of the heavy tanks, and we were ordered to put out a guard until a guard from our attached infantry came to relieve us, and to dig one slit trench per tank. I would have been quite content with the protection of my own tank's turret but dutifully passed on the orders, and sent Evan off to help Sergeant Harding dig a slit trench for the guard, who probably would need one. Mudie and I began to try and make some impression on the stony ground. The burning derelicts were no longer visible, and for the moment there was a background of profound quiet.

After we had been digging about a minute a projectile of some sort screamed over our heads and burst with an orange flame and a great deal of noise somewhere in the darkness behind us, apparently somewhere among the heavy tanks. Another followed it, and I decided that it would be ridiculous to attempt digging a trench under HE fire when the tank turret was already available for our protection. Evan came back from Sergeant Harding's tank and scrambled into the turret. I told Mudie to get in after him and as soon as they had made room stepped in myself, trying not to hurry too much. There was silence for the next two minutes and I began to wonder if I had made an ass of myself. Sergeant Harding's head appeared over the top of the turret. 'Here, Evan,' he said, 'What are you sulking in there for man? If you stop digging every time a bit of shit comes over we'll never get finished. Come on out of it now and do a bit of bloody work. There's no call to hop in the turret every time you get a bit of shit thrown at you.' 'All right,' I said, giving in to Sergeant Harding's greater experience, 'Get out and do some more digging.' Evan and I climbed out onto the engine plates at the back of the tank, and prepared to drop to the ground. But with a scream and a crash another shell arrived and burrowed into the earth about thirty yards off from us. Something glanced along the side of my boot and two or three more pieces hit on the side of the tank with a clang: Evan rolled sideways off the back of it and fell to the ground. 'Are you all right?' I asked him. 'Yes sir.' 'Well get back into the turret. I'm not going to muck about digging in this stuff.' To my considerable satisfaction I heard Sergeant Harding also ordering his men to take cover. He was not going to recant entirely however, but made them lie under the belly of the

tank and begin to scoop a trench there. As I started to climb up on
the tank again I put my hand on one of the two-gallon water-
containers in the rack behind the engine. It was still hot from the
exhaust so I climbed back onto the turret and said to Evan and
Mudie: 'I'm going to make some coffee from the hot water at
the back of the tank. You can stay there if you like but I'm going
underneath at the back.' Evan remained inside muttering something about not sticking his bloody neck out, but Mudie and I
were [underneath] the rear end of the tank before the next shell
arrived. There we lay, drinking warm, if somewhat silty coffee,
while the shelling continued irregularly — it was a solitary mortar
which plagued us — for the best part of an hour. In one of the
intervals I took a mug of coffee up to Evan, although I didn't wish
him luck with it.

Andrew came back from the Colonel's tank and sent me over
there to do a spell as duty officer during the night. I rolled up
my bedding, humped it onto my shoulders and followed his
directions until I found the great bulk of the Grant looking like a
castle in the moonlight. John Simpson of B Squadron had arrived
there on the same job, and I felt happier at seeing someone I
knew. He was still the youngest officer in the regiment after two
years, a tall thin chap with a tendency to sarcasm which increased
when he felt shy. He was an entertaining talker and made a point
of knowing about curious subjects such as the underground
activities of Jewish business concerns in England or ancient
Egyptian theology. He made some polite remark about being
glad to see me back and began to tell me how he had been
spending the evening in injecting morphia into our supporting
infantry most of whom by his account had crowded into the
turret of his Sherman when the shelling started. Some of the
shells had apparently landed among the infantry vehicles and
heavy tanks at the back of the leaguer. 'My tank is now a dressing
station,' he went on with a sort of carefully maintained mock
seriousness. Although at the time it seemed to me and I think to
all of us that we were carrying it off rather well, I realised
afterwards that to anyone who like a film audience could have
taken a detached view of us, our restraint would have been pretty
obvious. In Sergeant Harding's voice saying: 'There's no need to
hop in the turret every time' there was a higher, more excitable
note, an exaggeration of his usual Welsh singsong. In ordering
Evan and Mudie back into the turret I had enforced my orders
with two or three redundant blasphemies. And now John and I

continued in this awful vein of banter as we went to look for a place to put our beds.

There were one or two German infantry positions and pits for lorries to be driven into; deepcut and beautifully finished trenches. John had selected a deep and narrow trench about the right size for a single bed and was going to drop his bedding into it, when I said: 'I think there's some stuff in the bottom of it.' 'Oh.' John peered down into the murk. 'I hope it's not a corpse.' That was exactly why I had said 'Some stuff' instead of 'Something': but the object, whatever it was, was about the length of a man and in a pose which suggested limbs. I stretched a tentative and reluctant hand down into the pit wondering whether I should touch first the stiffened arm, the shoulder or the leg. I aimed at the centre of the mass to avoid contact with the face and teeth. Of course after all this agony it was not a corpse but someone else's bedding. We [had] been forestalled, and had to sleep in a pit dug for a small truck, where we put our beds side by side. When we had arranged them I walked back with John to his own tank. It was nearly double the size of my own, and impressed me that evening, seeing a Sherman for the first time, as a massively safe stronghold, although in a few days' time I would not have changed my lowbuilt comparatively fragile Crusader for it. On the towering side of it was painted a huge eye. 'The eye of Horus' said John. 'He's the nearest thing in Egyptian mythology to Mars. I put it on with sump oil and the black off a brew tin.'

We found two infantrymen still sheltering inside the tank although the shelling had been over for more than an hour. One of them explained quite plausibly that he was keeping his companion company; the companion being 'took real bad'. This at first I supposed to mean that he was seriously wounded, but in fact he was unhurt though badly shocked. We found a truck to take him away to the RAP and he was helped out and lowered down the front of the tank. The effects of morphia seemed to have left his head and nerve centres and concentrated in his legs which refused to support him. The infantry sentry who helped us get him down, disdaining John's device of banter, said honestly and plainly to me: 'I'll be glad when this is over, won't you, Sir?' While this was not a very clever or original thing to say, it was exactly what I was thinking and I agreed with him heartily. The exchange of banalities did us both good. By the time John and I had got back to our beds, after sharing a packet of chocolate, the British 25 pounders, spaced one to every twenty five yards behind us, had

opened a barrage which lasted most of the night. The noises of
the shells like those of aeroplane engines varied according to the
angle at which they struck the ear. One gun which appeared to be
firing directly over our heads sent a shell which whistled.
Possibly at some part of the night there was some enemy
counterbattery fire, or else some heavier guns of our own joined
in. At all events there was every variety of noise in the sky, a
whistling and chattering and rumbling of gigantic invisible trains;
noises like a person whispering into a microphone; and of tearing
cloth. The sky was lit up almost without pause by the great
flashes on the horizon, and the noise so continuous that we slept
easily beneath it. Once I woke providentially in time to prevent
the driver of a fifteen hundredweight truck which was coming
through the area from taking us and the pit in his stride.

I was lucky enough to have the last spell of duty — from one
o'clock until dawn. The duty officer had to wander about the area
visiting the guards and pickets; to deal with any messages
received over the air by the duty operator; to call the Colonel at
five o'clock and then rout the whole regimental group out of bed.
The infantry had a machine gun post out in front of the leaguer,
and when I visited them they reported a snipers' post somewhere
in front of us. The fifteen hundredweight which had almost run
over us had been one of a unit which had moved back during the
night after having several casualties. While we were talking of
this two bullets sang past in the darkness like innocuous insects:
one struck a tank somewhere and rebounded whining into the
darkness. At five o'clock I duly woke the Colonel, who lay in his
opulent sleeping bag, his clothes and suede boots neatly piled
beside him. A scent of pomade drifted from him as he sat up. I
was conscious that after a night in my clothes quite a different
scent was drifting from me. I told him the time and about the
snipers, and handed over to his batman who already hovered
behind me with a cup of tea, presumably made on a cooker in the
turret of one of the big tanks. I went about stirring the sleeping
cocoons of men with my foot. Passing John still slumbering in the
pit, I woke him and said: 'Have some whisky. I suppose we've
sunk pretty low, taking it for breakfast.' Unfortunately there was
no more chocolate.

By six o'clock the wireless in every tank was switched on,
engines were running, and at six fifteen, through a thick mist the
Crusader squadron began to move out in close formation ahead of
the regiment, gradually extending with the light. Andrew had had

relayed to me the vaguest orders; the only thing he seemed sure about was that there was no one between us and the enemy. If that were so it seemed crazy to go swanning off into the mist. But I was fairly certain it was untrue: and presently, as we moved forward keeping one eye on the vague shape of Andrew's tank in the mist to my left, I saw on my right a truck with its crew dismounted, reported it and went over to look at them. Of course it was a British truck, whose driver told me that there was a whole unit of soft vehicles ahead of us, and no enemy for a mile or so at least. There was no more talk of snipers and I imagined that they would have been part of some sort of patrol which had been withdrawn to the main German positions at first light. Andrew now began to call me fussily over the air: 'Nuts 5 Nuts 5 You're miles behind, come on Come on, Off.' Speeding up we saw the shape of a tank ahead of us again and made for it. It was a derelict. I had never thought of derelicts complicating manoeuvres in a bad light, but I was made to think of them again and again in the next quarter of an hour. We seemed to be crossing ground which had been fiercely contested. There seemed to be no one ahead of us and I began to suppose that we had passed Andrew in the mist; it was soon clear that we were lost, and had even lost our general sense of direction, being without a compass. It was a bad feeling. In fact, the regiment had made a sharp turn left while we were halted in conversation with the occupants of the truck, and if Andrew had thought to mention this to me over the air, I could have found them quite easily. As it was we continued to move nervously round until the mist cleared, Evan clutching a Tommy gun and I a revolver. Seeing some Crusaders when it grew clear enough to pick up objects at a distance, we made towards them. It was the Colonel and Regimental headquarters of one of the other regiments in the Brigade, but he had no idea on which side of him our regiment would be. How all this ignorance came about I am not sure, because I afterwards found Brigade and Regimental orders to be very clear, and in later actions every member of every tank crew had some idea of the whole set-up from the general's plan down to his own position and task. This was only the third time the Brigade had seen action as a tank Brigade, and the truth is I was probably not so much behind the others in experience as I had imagined.

So we rushed eagerly towards every Crusader we saw, like a short sighted dog that has got lost on the beach. Andrew went on calling us up unhelpfully with such messages as: 'Nuts 5 Nuts 5 I

still can't see you. Conform. Off.' I saw that two other tanks of the
squadron had attached themselves to us and were following us
slavishly about, although the other tank of my own troop was
nowhere to be seen. Another Crusader some hundreds of yards
away attracted out attention and we rushed towards it flounder-
ing over slit trenches and passing through some of our own
infantry. I was alert to avoid running the men in these trenches
over, but when we seemed clear of them I was too late to prevent
the driver from running over a man in black overalls who was
leaning on the parapet of a trench. A moment before the tank
crunched over him I realised he was already dead — the first dead
man I had ever seen. Looking back I saw he was a negro. 'Libyan
troops' said Evan in my ear. He was pointing. There were several
of them scattered about, their clothes soaked with dew; some
lacking limbs, although no flesh of these was visible, the clothes
seeming to have decently wrapped themselves round the places
where arms legs and even heads were missing, I have sometimes
noticed this before in photographs of people killed by explosive.

The Crusader that had attracted our attention was newly
painted, covered with bedding and kit [. . .]

As Douglas described in *Alamein to Zem Zem*, he fought
through to Mersa, then, after a pause there, went on with
his regiment to further fighting at El Agheila in Libya.
Christmas 1942 they spent near Nofilia, where some mail
got through including books from his mother. '[I have
heard] nothing from Blunden for months. It incenses me
that he should have his room stacked with review copies of
books which he doesn't want, by the hundred, and here we
are starved for books, and it never occurs to him to send
any. In fact I've even asked him twice, but he doesn't do
anything about it. You might like to see if you can chivvy
him into it.' Blunden had in fact been active on his behalf.

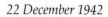

22 December 1942   *Merton College*

Dear Mrs Douglas, Thank you for your card; I was to write and
the new address is timely. I heard lately from Keith who had
received he mentioned 'a long letter' from me, and another is on
the way to him, but as you say the postman must find it hard to

catch him up. He sent several poems, and desired me to pass on one to you; I have a wish to try one on the *Times Lit^y Supp^t*, if you have not sent it elsewhere. Details at the end of this letter. His news was rather romantic, and I had a pleasant mention of him (perhaps with a hint of this romantic quality) in a letter from Hamo Sassoon, formerly of Merton. — Shortage of staff here and plenty of all sorts of duty have worn some of us down, our youthful bloom may be hard to recapture. At the moment we *are* in much anxiety over the illness of our old hero Professor Garrod. — Keith sent a magnificent Christmas picture, no doubt libellous, of a sort of staff officer announcing the Messiah in a very agitated manner, with trumpet. May he continue well and merry in spite of all, until the good day of his return.

With best respects   yours sincerely   *E. Blunden*

The poem is called *Devils*, but possibly you have tried it some-where? It begins

My mind's silence is not that of a wood
Warm and full of the sun's patience,

And he says he has altered it since sending you a copy.

to MRS DOUGLAS
7 January 1943   *Merton College*

I am glad to say that the editor of the Times Literary Supp^t will print K's poem 'Devils', and I am asking him to send the fee to you. Yes, I expect K's Christmas card was all his own work! and it shows, his spirit of Liberty is still on the wing. I have not heard again but hope you have or will soon.

Best respects,   Yours   *E. Blunden*

15 February 1943   *Merton College*

Dear Mrs Douglas,   I imagine you have heard from Keith, who writes to me (31 Jan.) from No. 1 General Hospital M.E.F., hoping that he will be out of it in 6 weeks. He was wounded by putting his foot under a trip wire which set off some bombs; and he had had some of the metal which hit him removed when he wrote. Apart from that he describes the campaign as 'interesting and instructive', but complains that his mail has been very elusive. He includes a transcript of a poem 'Waiting for an

Offensive' ['The Offensive'], which is to my mind a very keen impression of that silent crisis.

Thank you for your letter, and the poem ['The Knife'?] — I hope I shall have the pleasure of seeing you here as you mention at the end of the week.   Yours sincerely   *E. Blunden*

To MRS DOUGLAS
7 March 1943   *Merton College*

Very glad to have your summary of the latest news from Keith, who collects the slings and arrows of fortune so cheerfully — I will pack him up something to read though he will not find very much of great merit going on now. I wish his idea may prove right, and his return be not too far off, but these Wars are unpredictable. But we do not lack prophets, — only I think their mathematics are very elementary. I will try the T.L.S. again with verse by K. as soon as something comes which seems to suit their general drift. Best respects,   *E. Blunden*

To KEITH DOUGLAS
17 May 1943

I am submitting copies of 'Traps for Words' ['Words'] and 'The Regimental Trumpeter' ['The Trumpet'] to the Times Lit. Supp. 'Landscape with Figures' is striking, but they ask for shorter pieces. Excuse a card, but I have little to report, and you will not want a description of *this* landscape with figures. I hope you are safe and sound, in good spirits in spite of the long time away. No doubt you have a pretty full life — and probably plenty of chance to use several languages. Perhaps you have received a communication or two from me though tardy.

Best luck,   *E. Blunden*

The poems were among several Douglas had written while in hospital and convalescing. At the beginning of May he rejoined his regiment outside Enfidaville, but saw no more of the fighting before the campaign's end. For a couple of months he remained in Tunisia. His earlier work had been appearing belatedly in England: *Eight Oxford Poets* (June

1942) — for which his mother received a royalty of £1.9.5d; Hall's *Selected Poems* (February 1943) — which sold virtually all its 2,000 copies in six months.

A new outlet for his work had appeared. Tambimuttu came across Douglas's work in *Fords and Bridges*; impressed by a couple of the Oxford poems published in it in May 1939, he sought Douglas out. Finally he managed to contact Mrs Douglas in July 1942, and asked her permission to include poems both in *Poetry (London)* and the yearly anthologies he was compiling for Faber and Faber. He also asked to see any future poems she received.

Tambimuttu proved his commitment by publishing work by Douglas each month in *Poetry (London)*. 'The Offensive', his third appearance, was in the January 1943 issue. 'Devils' was published in the *TLS*, 23 January 1943. Perhaps the gap between the earlier poems which had been appearing in England and the work he had written since experiencing action encouraged Douglas to take on the role of spokesman once more.

Poets in This War
(?May 1943)

I think it is true to say that of the poets who are now regarded as poets of the last war, the majority are writers whom the war inspired to their finest efforts, often to what may be regarded as their first efforts, and they are all soldiers.

The Great War was entered upon by us in a spirit of terrific conceit and was the culmination of a complacent period; so complacent that Kipling, although he was partly responsible for this mood, had some years before written a dignified and conditional warning 'Lest We Forget'.

The retreat from Mons, the aggregate of new horrors, the muddling generalship, the obsolescence of the gentleman in war demanded and obtained a new type of writing to comment on them (surprisingly perhaps to those who assess our national character). Rupert Brooke, who might have seemed our ready made herald and bard, appeared superannuated in a moment and wandered away fittingly, from a literary point of view, to die in a region of dead heroes. Instead, arose Owen, to the sound of wheels crunching the bones of a man scarcely dead; Sassoon's

tank lumbered into the music hall in the middle of a patriotic
song, Sorley and Isaac Rosenberg were hypnotized among all the
dangers by men and larks singing. Such was the jolt given to the
whole conception men had had of the world and of war, and so
clear was the nature of the cataclysm, that it was natural enough
not only that poets should be stirred, but that they should know
how to express themselves.

During the period 'entre deux guerres' we were listening
alternately to an emphasis of the horrible nature of modern war
and to the vague remedies of social and political reformers. The
nation's public character remained, in spite of all, as absurdly
ignorant and reactionary as ever.

Those who wrote of war looked back to the last even when they
spoke of the next, which was a bogy to frighten children and
electors with: the poets who were still at the height of their fame
before this war, who were accustomed to teach politics and even
supposed themselves, and were supposed, versed in the horrors
of the current struggles in Spain, were curiously unable to react to
a war which began and continued in such a disconcerting way.

The long inaction on all fronts was not inspiring; everyone was
too used to inaction. Dunkirk was over almost before most people
had rubbed the sleep out of their eyes; inaction, as far as most
soldiers were concerned, began again. This produced, as it was
bound to, an amount of loitering, fed-up poetry, vaguely relat-
able to some of Turner's poems 1914-18.

So far I have not mentioned the name of a poet 'of the present
war'. I might refuse to on the grounds that it is unnecessary: for I
do not find even one who stands out as an individual. It seems
there were no poets at Dunkirk; or if there were, they stayed
there. Instead we have had poetic pioneers and land girls in the
pages (respectively) of *New Writing* and *Country Life*. There have
been desperately intelligent conscientious objectors, R.A.M.C.
orderlies, students. In the fourth year of this war we have not a
single poet who seems likely to be an impressive commentator on
it.

In England, Henry Treece is now the head of some sort of
poetic school; of what kind I am not sure. John Hall, from the
headquarters of the International Art Club in London, is writing
very involved verses with an occasional oblique and clever
reference to bombs or bullets. *Poetry (London)* is edited by one
Tambimuttu; his uniform, if he has one, is probably exotic. John
Lehmann is encouraging the occupants of British barrack rooms

to work off their repressions in his pages. Of *Horizon* I know nothing up to date: what I do know answers the trend of these remarks. There are a number of very young men, sprung up among the horrors of War Time Oxford, some of whom, notably Sidney Keyes, are technically quite competent but have no experiences worth writing of.

John Heath Stubbs, who published some of the decade's worst printed verse in *Eight Oxford Poets*, their subjects are either escapist or as I believe evidence of lack of material, has written a long poem called 'Wounded Thamuz'. Their attitude to the war is that of the homosexual Guardsman returning from Dunkirk — 'Oh my dear! the noise! and the people!' They turn a delicate shoulder to it all. But no paper shortage stems the production of hundreds of slim volumes and earnestly compiled anthologies of wartime poetry, *Poems From the Forces*, &c. Above all there are a hundred shy little magazines, whose contributors are their most ardent supporters. Benevolent publishers, it seems, are constantly patting blushing young poets on the head (I am tempted to use blushing as Masefield does) and encouraging them to lisp in numbers.

The Middle East is the only theatre of war which is employing or has been employing large numbers of English soldiers for a long time, in active warfare; here the veterans of Greece and Crete have merged with the more recently experienced desert soldiers. Here too are magazines which rashly encourage embryo poets. *Gen* and *Orientations* and an occasional quarter page of *Parade* welcome their effusions: and receive them, from clerks and staff officers who have too little to do, and from the back end of the desert army. The poets who wrote so much and so well before the war, all over the world, find themselves silenced, or able to write on almost any subject but war. Why did all this happen? Why are there no poets like Owen and Sassoon who lived with the fighting troops and wrote of their experiences while they were enduring them?

The reasons are psychological, literary, military and strategic, diverse. There are such poets, but they do not write. They do not write because there is nothing new, from a soldier's point of view, about this war except its mobile character. There are two reasons: hell cannot be let loose twice: it was let loose in the Great War and it is the same old hell now. The hardships, pain and boredom; the behaviour of the living and the appearance of the dead, were so accurately described by the poets of the Great War that everyday on the battlefields of the western desert — and no doubt on the Russian battlefields as well — their poems are illustrated. Almost all that a modern poet on active service is inspired to write, would be tautological. And the mobility of modern warfare does not give the same opportunities for writing as the long routines of trench warfare. The poets behind the line are not war poets, in the sense of soldier poets, because they do not have the soldier's experience at first hand. English civilians have not endured any suffering comparable to that of other European civilians, and England has not been heavily bombed long enough for that alone to produce a body of 'war' poetry.

Nor can we produce a body of long range poetry inspired by shocking news items. The poet at home can only make valuable comments on social and political issues, which he may do more easily, both because he can see more clearly and because the censor will be more lenient with him, in retrospect.

Meanwhile the soldiers have not found anything new to say. Their experiences they will not forget easily, and it seems to me that the whole body of English war poetry of this war, civil and military, will be created after war is over.

1 June 1943   *Notts SR Yeo MEF*

Dear Tambimuttu,   I have just received a letter from a secretary of yours whose name is illegible: she includes a memo of one Schooling whom I connect with rancid butter, as possibly he can explain; and a request for poems. I am sending you some. There are more, if I hear that you have received these and want more. I think you had better write and ask Mr Edmund Blunden if any of these have been used by the Times Lit. Supp. Copies were sent him some time ago: please send him the ones you don't want, anyway, in case he never received them.

I may have written some more by the time I next hear from you, but, enfin Tunisia, like Grishkin, is nice, and it is amazing what you can get for a tin of bully beef from a hungry civilian population. I am hoping to use some as rent and move in on a family, in which case I shall be busy. Anyway, there must be some leave, somewhere. Such things must be after a famous victoree.

    Yours   *Keith Douglas*

To JOHN HALL
10 June 1943   *Notts SR Yeo MEF*

Dear John,   I am having a hell of a good time in Tunisia, which is
the best country I've struck yet, particularly as one gets towards
Algeria. My French is ungrammatical but fluent and is a great
help. I bathe 3 or 4 times a day in more or less Bermudan Waters (I
wish I had a glass boat), and we have very amiable dances and
parties now and then. You have been making cutting remarks
about my poems for so long I ought to retaliate but I haven't seen
any of yours for a long time, except here and there. The nastiest
and truest thing I can say is that you are getting too involved and
precious, chiefly because you now find yourself in a backwater
and have nothing to write about that is relevant. The same
applied to me in pre-Alamein days and I reacted differently but if
anything produced worse. With regard to your criticisms of my
stuff, I think you are beginning to condemn all that is not your
own favourite brand, and are particularly anti réportage and
extrospective (if the word exists) poetry — which seems to me the
sort that has to be written just now, even if it is not attractive.
Mother sent me some copies of female psycho-analyst reviews of
my work which made me retch; and described that shit Spender's
efforts. I gave 2 offficers a lift the other day and they turned out to
be an old schoolfellow of mine and friend of yours, Geoff.
Wagner, and Richard Green Valley Llewellyn Lloyd. I've not
seen our book yet. Write again soon   *Keith*

In a letter of 10 October 1942 Hall had written to Mrs
Douglas that he was sending 'Christodoulos' and 'Egypt' on
to Tambimuttu: 'I must admit that I do not like them at all.
Keith has yet to surpass the excellence of his early poems.
These poems from abroad seem to lack the emotional and
intellectual validity of his best work and it is a pity that he
cannot relax into a simpler expression of his thoughts and
feelings. He seems to me to be writing too remotely, cleverly
but not movingly. You may pass on these remarks to Keith if
you like; he will know they come from a friendly critic.'
Sending back the copies to Mrs Douglas on 1 November,
after Tambimuttu had returned them, Hall added: 'as I feel
no great enthusiasm for them I wont bother to send them

elsewhere.' On 10 August Hall's criticisms would bear unexpected fruit.

❧

26 June 1943   *Notts SR Yeo MEF*

Dear John, This is such a bloody pen that I shall write in pencil after all. I have at last received a copy of Selected Poems and of PL, and — by the hand of Geoff. Wagner, Sheila Shannon's review in the Spectator. First of all, Selected Poems. It is a handsome little pamphlet, though it would have a longer life in a paper cover than in that ridiculous cardboard, the back of which comes off after a few hours. I like the type and the presentation of the poems. On the selection, Norman Nicholson appears the best of us — which perhaps he is, being the eldest. I think a few more biographical details might have been given in front. I don't think you were fair to yourself, but you know best what is best of yours. I particularly like Walking to Westminster and Journey to London and Earthbound. I would say Elegy on a hill, but it puzzled me a bit, though the feeling of it is impressive, that is to say the feeling it gives and the feelings I suppose you had when you wrote it. I think you need a little more cynicism, or should I say indifference to emotion once felt, in your poetic make-up. I am getting at the same thing as the Shannon bitch (bitch for what she said about me). You are too much affected. I don't want that you should lose the sensitiveness, or even some of it. But that you should be deeply affected, and yet not show it so much — a little more of the traditional Englishman — however much you deplore him — would make your poetry stronger and more impressive. I think the selection you have made of me is surprisingly near what I'd have made myself. I am glad you put in Caravan, although I don't think Famous Men *and* Images were *both* necessary. I wish the dates of all these poems could have been put on them, as it would have made it easier for reviewers not to talk cock about them. By the way, although you discovered a piece of gammy syntax in The Marvel, and corrected it, some one has made nonsense of a verse of the Villanelle, (which was correctly printed in Augury), and complete nonsense, by changing one word, of The Prisoner (this has also, as I should expect, been done by Tambimuttu). The verse in the Villanelle reads, in your printing. 'Birds feel the enchantment of his wing (whose wing?)/and in ten fine notes dispel 20 cares.' I wrote 'Bird feels the enchantment of his (bird's) wing/& . . . dispels . . .' I am sorry if the omission of the definite article misled you. The point of the Prisoner is that the ambitious cruel bone is the prisoner, who wishes to escape the bright flesh and emerge into fulfilment as a skeleton. 'There was the urge (to break the bright flesh and emerge) OF the ambitious cruel bone.' There is no question of escaping from the bone. I know its unavoidable at such a distance, but it's annoying. Finally, if you happen to know S. Shannon, point out that the meaningless phrase she cites is used with intent and the words carefully chosen. I shall write to her myself, not so much to correct her as to make her acquaintance & correct her in future. I am also writing to Tambi to say I am *Not* in the Tank Corps (which is a formation which doesn't exist).

cheerio   *Keith*

I should be very interested to see any other copies of Poetry London.

26 June 1943   *Notts SR Yeo MEF*

Dear John,   I have written you a long lettercard all about Selected Poems, which I have at last received and which I liked. Thank you very much for all you have done towards keeping me in print in England. I'm sorry Sheila Shannon didn't agree with you that it was worth it. Anyway she gave you and Norman a write-up.

Did you ever receive the poems I wrote in hospital? I am not likely to produce anything but virtual repetitions of these, until the war is cleared up now, because I doubt if I shall be confronted with any new horrors or any worse pain, short of being burnt up, which I am not likely to survive. With which cheerful thought my space is exhausted.   *Keith*

[Written on the endpapers of Douglas's copy of *Selected Poems* and heavily crossed out by him, an early draft of 'Vergissmeinnicht':]

A Dead Gunner

Three weeks since pierced by flung metal
the sound steel broke beside my belly

[drew us back shattered]: the turret in a flurry
of blood and Bilby quite still, dribbling spittle,

and we advanced and knocked out that gun
and the crew got away somehow
to skulk in the mountains until now
the campaign over. [But] they left one,

they left you, perhaps the boy
to whom Steffi had written Vergissmeinnicht
on this photograph in the ditch. Perhaps the hand
that gave Evans and Bilby their last gift

For we see you with a sort of content
Abased, seeming to have paid
mocked by your own durable equipment
the metal beneath your decaying head undecayed.

Yet she would weep to see how you are fallen away
and on your back the great blow flies move
and the dust gathering in your paper eye
your stomach open in a stinking cave.

Yes here the lover and the killer lie mingled
for the two have but one body and one heart
and death that had the cruel soldier singled
out, has done the lover mortal hurt.

Tunisia 1943

postmark: 28 June 1943   *Poetry (London)*

Dear Douglas, Many thanks for your poems Gallantry, Words,
Desert Flowers, Landscape with Figures [sent on 1 June]. I like
them. Will print them in *Poetry* and in two anthologies I am
compiling Poems from the Services (Nicholson & Watson) and
Poetry in Wartime II (Faber) [neither appeared]. Meanwhile could
you continue to send me your new poems as they arrive and I will
return those I don't want to Mr Blunden. Payments for your poems
will be made to your mother.

Also would you care to make a selection of your poems for

possible publication by PL (Nicholson & Watson) in book form? I
think a book by you would be interesting. I hope you will include
as many M.E. poems as possible.

Yours   *Tambimuttu*

[PS] Will give your message to Schooling!

[*11 July 1943*]   *Notts SR Yeo MEF*

Dear Tambimuttu, Thank you for your letter, and for publishing
my poems — I had given up all idea of writing in the Army until
your efforts and John Hall's nerved me to try again. I'll go on
sending you poems as they come — I send you one, ARISTO-
CRATS, with this. But sometimes there are very long gaps. I
would very much like to publish a selection of my poems in book
form: but I would like it to be in my own selection, and so if you
want me to do that would you let me know how many poems
you'd want, and let me have a list of titles of all my poems which
you or my mother or Edmund Blunden have in England. I would
certainly include plenty of M.E. poems and would like to write 3
or 4 pages of introduction. If you want any articles on poetry I
could send you one or two — for instance one on the lack of
Owens, Sassoons etc in this war.

Yours   *Keith Douglas*

Aristocrats

The noble horse with courage in his eye,
clean in the bone, looks up at a shellburst:
away fly the images of the shires
but he puts the pipe back in his mouth.

Peter was unfortunately killed by an 88;
it took his leg away, he died in the ambulance.
I saw him crawling on the sand, he said
It's most unfair, they've shot my foot off.

How can I live among this gentle
obsolescent breed of heroes, and not weep?
Unicorns, almost,

for they are fading into two legends
in which their stupidity and chivalry
are celebrated. Each, fool and hero, will be an immortal.

These plains were their cricket pitch
and in the mountains the tremendous drop fences
brought down some of the runners. Here then
under the stones and earth they dispose themselves,
I think with their famous unconcern.
It is not gunfire I hear, but a hunting horn.

Tunisia 1943

[Letterhead: Governo Generale della Libia/Comando Superiore
Forze Armate della Libia/Quartiere Generale. Inscribed by KD at
the top: W IL DUCE/W IL RE/RITORNEREMO/VINCEREMO DUCE.]
11 July 1943

Dear Tambimuttu, Thank you for your airgraph, and suggestion
that I should make a selection to appear in book form. This I
should be glad to do. I've written you an airgraph in reply to that,
but as they say overseas mail is quicker than airgraphs now I'm
writing a letter. If I make a selection someone would have to send
me a list of titles of poems which you or my mother or Edmund
Blunden have now, because I can't really remember all that exist
— I had completely forgotten writing the last poem in John Hall's
selection of my stuff. As to including a lot of ME stuff, there isn't
as yet a very great deal to include; because I like to write in
comfort or not at all and the nearest to comfort available most of
the time is not near enough. A few flies are enough to destroy my
inspiration, if they keep on the job the way Egyptian, Tripolitanian
and Tunisian flies do. What I have written has been written in
hospitals, Con. depots, Base depots etc — emotion recollected in
tranquillity — and as I'm now living in a hole in the sand with a
piece of canvas over it, in the inadequate shade of a palm tree, I
don't expect to be very creative. I am angling for the job of Brigade
Entertainment Officer while we are sitting around, which would
enable me to live in a house, with my own room and a vehicle at
my disposal. If I get the job I'll send you bags of literature, in all
forms and on all subjects. On the back of this I have rewritten a
poem I sent you by airgraph ['Aristocrats'] in case the airgraph is
illegible.
  Yrs. *Keith D.*

To J. C. HALL (incomplete)
10 August 1943

. . . Incidentally you say I fail as a poet, when you mean I fail as a lyricist. Only someone who is out of touch, by which I mean first hand touch, with what has happened outside England — and from a cultural point of view I wish it had affected English life more — could make that criticism. I am surprised you should still expect me to produce musical verse. A lyric form and a lyric approach will do even less good than a journalese approach to the subjects we have to discuss now. I don't know if you have come across the word Bullshit — it is an army word and signifies humbug and unnecessary detail. It symbolizes what I think must be got rid of — the mass of irrelevancies, of 'attitudes', 'approaches', propaganda, ivory towers, etc., that stands between us and our problems and what we have to do about them.

To write on the themes which have been concerning me lately in lyrical and abstract forms, would be immense bullshitting. In my early poems I wrote lyrically, as an innocent, because I was an innocent: I have (not surprisingly) fallen from that particular grace since then. I had begun to change during my second year at Oxford. T. S. Eliot wrote to me when I first joined the army, that I appeared to have finished with one form of writing and to be progressing towards another, which he did not think I had mastered. I knew this to be true, without his saying it. Well, I am still changing: I don't disagree with you if you say I am awkward and not used to the new paces yet. But my object (and I don't give a damn about my duty as a poet) is to write true things, significant things in words each of which works for its place in a line. My rhythms, which you find enervated, are carefully chosen to enable the poems to be *read* as significant speech: I see no reason to be either musical or sonorous about things at present. When I do, I shall be so again, and glad to. I suppose I reflect the cynicism and the careful absence of expectation (it is not quite the same as apathy) with which I view the world. As many others to whom I have spoken, not only civilians and British soldiers, but Germans and Italians, are in the same state of mind, it is a true reflection. I never tried to write about war (that is battles and things, not London can Take it), with the exception of a satiric picture of some soldiers frozen to death, until I had experienced it. Now I will write of it, and perhaps one day cynic and lyric will meet and make me a balanced style. Certainly you will never see the long metrical similes and galleries of images again.

Your talk of regrouping sounds to me — if you will excuse me for exhibiting a one-track mind — like the military excuse of a defeated general. There is never much need to regroup. Let your impulses drive you forward; never lose contact with life or you will lose the impulses as well. Meanwhile if you must regroup, do it by re-reading your old stuff.

Of course, you will never take my advice nor I yours. But in these tirades a few ideas do scrape through the defences on either side. Perhaps all this may make it easier for you to understand why I am writing the way I am and why I shall never go back to the old forms. You may even begin to see some virtue in it. To be sentimental or emotional now is dangerous to oneself and to others. To trust anyone or to admit any hope of a better world is criminally foolish, as foolish as it is to stop working for it. It sounds silly to say work without hope, but it can be done; it's only a form of insurance; it doesn't mean work hopelessly.   [Keith]

To EDMUND BLUNDEN
12 August [1943]   Notts SR Yeo MEF

The Sniper

Under the parabola of a ball
a child, turning into a man,
I looked into the air too long.
The ball fell in my hand. It sang
in the closed fist: Open, Open.
Behold a gift, designed to kill.

In my dial of glass appears
the soldier who is going to die.
He smiles, and moves about in ways
his mother knows, habits of his;
the wires touch his face. I cry
NOW. Death, like a familiar, hears

and look, has made a man of dust,
from a live man. This sorcery
I do: being damned, I am amused

> to see the centre of love diffused;
> the waves of love travel into vacancy;
> how easy it is to be a ghost.
>
> The weightless mosquito touches
> her tiny shadow on the stone
> and with how like, how infinite
> a lightness, man and shadow meet.
> They fuse. A shadow is a man
> When the mosquito death approaches.

Is THE SNIPER ['How to Kill'] any good to you? Incidentally NOW in verse 3 is meant to be in capitals. Have just written you a letter. Best wishes.   *Keith*

16 August 1943   *Merton College*

My dear Keith, I don't think all my cards have reached you, — I am sorry to have written cards but felt dull occasionally and had little to say, — this condition being probably due to Wars and such, although I lurk here, as C. Smart says 'in thankful safety'. Your letter of 12 July is received and I delight to know that you and Hamo are, or were, once more neighbours. It is such a long time since you went forth, but I hope it will afterwards be a deep source of inspiration and subject, — even though a great deal of the theme must be painful and perplexed. The fighting man in this as in other wars is at least the only man whom Truth really cares to meet.

Be sure I have had no glooms at all over your keeping in touch with John Hall, as one of your contemporaries in poetical action — I am all for it. Anything that he can do to make your poems known suits me. — I wonder if you are becoming a little pre-occupied with the dry Ironic — the piece you transcribe, 'Aristocrats', is excellent that way, but that way is not the strongest for the sense of the acute reader and misses the general reader. I would like to see you writing with a fullness of music and a broadness of understanding, so as to bring us all into the circle. Again, forgive my Antiquity, but I am struck by Matthew Arnold, W. Owen, W. Shakespeare (Sonnets) and some others who evade irony and give a harmony of emotions.

This means, *let go more*! and *that* means, let the bigger flow of poetry carry your moods more. Well, I don't know how to express it, so bob down from your bombardment with old Italian wine-bottles, portraits of Dorando and D'Annunzio, and perhaps of Il Duce.

Sheila Shannon of the *Spectator* is slightly known to me. I expect she would find your poems too sharp-angled, but can't tell.

The photographs will go on to your Mother, and I am glad you let me see them. The 9 New Zealanders who took that eyrie and held it were No Ordinary Men. Neither are you to have a bed just against the wheels of railway engines. If you had not told me I should have thought Milena was of Somerville. Perhaps she was hiding something from you.

— 'Frank Phillips reading it.' We should have won long ago if his vocal efforts could have removed mountains, panzer divisions etc. But as he is an Old Blue you and I should be suitably impressed.

I have little local news worth transport, — nothing much happens except organization. The Cadet Courses form a temporary University. Prof. Garrod keeps up a gentle Social Scene. The notice NO BEER occurs about the town.

Best wishes from Sylva and me,   Yours ever *Edmund*

23 August 1943   *Merton College*

Dear Mrs Douglas, This is only to bring you some striking Photographs which Keith wished to come on to you. His 'bed's head' reminds me of those natural history stories, of swallows nesting in blast furnaces etc. I am glad he sounds so lively and equal to all that chances: and that he is not neglected by contemporary poets, and perhaps publishers.

With best respects   Yours sincerely   *E. Blunden*

3 September 1943   *Notts SR Yeo MEF*

Dear Edmund, No news since I last wrote to send you the photographs. I don't think you have seen this poem [presumably 'Vergissmeinnicht'] — or at least, not the revised version. I am afraid it may be a bit grisly for T.L.S.: but on the other hand not 'clever' enough for Tambimuttu and his clan. What I am aiming at is a series of pretty simple pictures. The first of this kind was 'Christodoulos' — I don't know if you had it. Mother has a copy if you didn't see it.

I am sitting at Base Depot before rejoining the unit, having just had a course in sunny Palestine, interspersed with some pleasant week-ends among the modern architecture and other modern amenities of Tel Aviv. One who fought on the German side at Cambrai is of opinion that the German Army of this war will crack very suddenly.

I wish I believed him. Yrs   *Keith*

21 October 1943   *Merton College*

Just had your letter and the poem which I think your best concerning present subjects: I will see what happens, but certainly if not now, later on will be a season for a collection of such pieces. So proceed as topics appear (and leisure.) There is not much news here, and if your friend from Cambrai 26 years ago proves right we shan't grumble. Poor Stibbe (you remember him?) is one who will not return — he died, in a difficult little action which he met with his usual coolness, in Burma. D. Grant was in hospital in Sicily when last heard of. There's to be a new vol. of poems soon from C. Day Lewis, but the bards are not over active. I wish this may find you making up for the rest —

Best luck — *E. Blunden*

Coming to the end of his time in the Middle East, but with the possibility of securing a staff post there — it did not materialize in time — Douglas wrote to his mother with thoughts for his future. The letter does not survive but a letter from Blunden makes clear the direction of those thoughts.

15 November 1943   *12 Woodstock Close, Oxford*

Dear Mrs Douglas, I've lately written to Keith, a letter not one of my postcards though I find myself often reduced to that brevity. As for his questions about Oxford, I should be very glad if you would consult the Senior Tutor at Merton — Mr Deane Jones —

for he has the official information and a clear mind; I am no longer a Fellow etc, having resolved to use my powers and time so far as I can on my literary work and perhaps something specially connected with these times. But I imagine that the College will continue to pay Exhibitions, and that Groups will be presently considered as an equivalent to some part of Finals. If Keith does not give up his British Council idea it might work: I'd of course recommend him, though I suspect they are a rather cautious Body and want 'safe' people rather than remarkable ones. But all the languages he can acquire will form a strong qualification. He *might* by means of them and general experience get a post as *Times* correspondent in the Middle East or elsewhere. May he be spared too much more of front line war. I, with you, don't like thinking too much on the prospects mentioned by Mr Churchill. But as you say some other course of events may appear, and usually this war 'some other' has. I well understand what you feel — And what he does when parcels arrive which have been rifled by the lads somewhere out of the battle.

　　With best respects　　Yours sincerely　　*E. Blunden*

[*?October 1943*]

Dear Edmund, I was very greatly glad to get a full length letter from you. I expect the war will no longer be getting you down so much as the peace. Poor old Beveridge; he will be no match for all these profit seeking reactionary shits, I am afraid. I could, in common with most members of all three services, go on about that for several pages; but the result would only reach you as a mass of excisions.

　　I am now able to get into Cairo occasionally although I still live in primitive conditions. I see a good deal of various poets whose names may have reached you — Bernard Spencer, Terence Tiller, Robin Fedden and occasionally Larry Durrell [from *Personal Landscape*]. In the opposite camp [i.e. *Salamander*] lie (and lie and lie) [. . .] and that dirty, inky little wretch [. . .]. I think he grows watercress in his ears, which are always full of rich Nile mud.

　　At the moment this whole côterie of bards [. . .] is quite overturned by the entry into it of a seventeen year old ex silk stocking maker, called Penny, who has told lies to the Army and is thought by the ATS to be of age. She has evidently been a prodigious reader and can join in our literary discussions with

zest although she makes some pretty startling remarks at times.
Her views on sex are revolutionary and all too frequently aired.
Her conduct however has nothing to do with them. But of course
none of this could have produced the explosion without the most
dangerous element, her beauty. In four days she had us all off our
feed, alternately sighing and glaring jealously at one another: and
has now departed for Palestine, much in the manner of ZULEIKA
DOBSON taking the train to Cambridge. Unfortunately for us all
she is coming back. Of which I suppose more news in my next.

As it is fast getting too dark to see the keyboard, and as I can't
type without seeing it I shall go on, (and as there is no news
anyway), to type out three poems, which I have sent on airgraphs
to Tambimuttu, who will probably find them illegible.

This Is the Dream

The shadows of leaves falling like minutes.
Seascapes. Discoveries of sea creatures
and voices out of the extreme distance reach us
like conjured sounds. Faces that are spirits

cruise across the backward glance of the brain.
In the bowl of the mind is pot-purri
Such shapes and hues become a lurid
décor to The Adventures. These are a cycle. When

I play dancer's choreographer's critic's role
I see myself dance happiness and pain
(each as illusory as rain)
in silence. Silence. Break it with the small

tinkle. The apathetic buzz buzz
pirouetting into a crescendo, BANG.   Until
as each scene closes hush the stage is still
everything is where it was.

The finale if it should come is

the moment my love and I meet
our hands reach out across a room of strangers
certain they hold the rose of love.

[Beside stanza three Douglas notes: 'The mixture as before, really.']

Enfidaville

In the church fallen like dancers
lie the virgin and St. Thérèse
on little pillows of dust.
The detonations of the last few days
tore down the ornamental plasters
shivered the hands of Christ.

The men and women who moved like candles
in and out of the houses and the streets
are all gone. The white houses are bare
black cages. No one is left to greet
the ghosts tugging at doorhandles
opening doors that are not there.

Now the daylight coming in from the fields
like a labourer, tired and sad,
is peering about among the wreckage, goes
past some corners as though with averted head
not looking at the sorrow this town holds
seeing no one move behind the windows.

But already they are coming back to search
like ants among their debris, finding in it
a bed or a piano and carrying it out.
Who would not love them at this minute?
I seem again to meet
the blue eyes of the images in the church.

I don't expect you to like this is the dream much, and I'm not
sure that I do myself, but it seemed just good enough not to scrap,
and certainly nothing more can be done with it. The one I enjoyed
writing most was of course the behaviour of fish.

Have you come across the poems of Louis Aragon? And what
do you think of them. Cyril Connolly goes off the deep end much
too easily about anyone he thinks he has discovered but all the
same I think 'there is something there'.

> Mon patrie est comme une barque
> Qu'abandonnèrent ses haleurs
> Et je ressemble à ce monarque

> Plus malheureux que le malheur
> Qui restait roi ses douleurs.

I wish I could be as neat as that

> Mon amour j'étais dans tes bras
> Au dehors quelqu'un murmura
> Une vieille chanson de France
> Mon mal enfin s'est reconnu
> Et son refrain comme un pied nu
> Troubla l'eau verte du silence.

Everyone chooses that one apparently, but I like it too. Probably if I knew enough about French literature I should know it had all been done by someone else before. If so I'm glad of my ignorance. Love to Sylva.

à bientôt   *Keith*   (Fish over the page)

Behaviour of fish in an Egyptian teagarden

As a white stone draws down the fish
she on the seafloor of the afternoon
draws down men's glances and their cruel wish
for love. Slyly her red lip on the spoon

slips-in a morsel of ice-cream: her hands
white as a milky stone, white submarine
fronds, sink with spread fingers, lean
along the table, carmined at the ends.

A cotton magnate, an important fish
with great eyepouches and a golden mouth
through the frail reefs of furniture swims out
and idling, suspended, stays to watch.

A crustacean old man clamped to his chair
sits coldly near her, and might see
her charms through fissures where the eyes should be
or else his teeth are parted in a stare.

Captain on leave, a lean dark mackerel
lies in the offing, turns himself and looks
through currents of sound. The flat-eyed flatfish sucks
on a straw, staring from its repose, laxly.

And gallants in shoals swim up and lag
circling and passing near the white attraction;
sometimes pausing, opening a conversation.
Fish pause so, to nibble and tug.

Now the ice-cream is finished, is
paid for. The fish swim off on business
and she sits alone at the table, a white stone
useless except to a collector, a rich man.

On 17 November Douglas embarked for Britain to arrive in mid December and enjoy three weeks leave. Blunden, it seems, had not yet heard of his departure.

8 January 1944   *Oxford*

I don't quite know where we are in correspondence (my side doesn't deserve that name) but just send you a shout. You last reported a 'côterie of bards' and the effects on these serious men of one Penny. I await the next. I don't mean, *a*ffects on me! Your Fish story in verse was ingenious. 'Poor Fish' is the only word except in the higher criticism. Well drawn. I often wonder if you are able to use your Pencil as well as pen now. — But since you wrote, of course all leisure may have vanished: I hope not. The early year seems to breathe promise, and I have refused to listen to Thomas Hardy on such occasions. — Best luck to you in all you do. — You didn't know F. H. Merk, I think, of C. H., my old master: he is gone at last.

Yours ever   *E. Blunden*

Of the three stories which follow, the first was written from Douglas's 1940 experiences at the Army Equitation School, Weedon, and published in *Lilliput* in July 1944. (It had previously appeared in *Citadel*, Cairo, July 1942.) The other two stories he submitted to the same magazine. They were returned on 27 March 1944, with the comment: 'Both of these stories are slightly too concerned with the horrific for us to be able to publish them straight after 'The Horse'.' Douglas then sent them to *Horizon*. On 8 June 1944, the stories were returned: 'We find them well and vigorously written and certainly very interesting although they are not quite suitable for this magazine.' 'Giuseppe', which is published here for the first time, was written some time after May 1943, when the incident it describes took place. 'The Little Red Mouth', which first appeared in *Stand* in 1970, was dated by Douglas 'Beni Yusef 1943'. Douglas was there around September/October 1943. The central incident of the story recurs in *Alamein to Zem Zem*. In January 1944 Douglas wrote to Tambimuttu that he had four stories about the Middle East 'so far written'. These two are all that survive.

Death of a Horse
(LILLIPUT, July 1944)

They stopped talking when the horse was led out. An orderly in a white coat led it out. One of its legs was broken, and the horse hobbled, almost hopped. Its expression was resigned and humble. It stood there, and they all stood there, looking at it with different thoughts in their minds. I expect, if you could have known what they were thinking, you could have told their characters.

Simon was thinking all the time: 'I wonder if it knows,' and after a time he thought: 'It does know, but it doesn't seem to mind.' Then the veterinary major came; he went into the shed and came out again with a clean white coat over his uniform, and a piece of chalk in one hand.

'You're lucky to see this,' he said. 'The last lot didn't have the chance.' He talked in a matter-of-fact way about an everyday occurrence. The horse stood there quietly, looking straight in front of it. As the vet moved to take hold of the headstall, it stumbled awkwardly, trying to shift to a more comfortable position.

'I draw a line from here to here,' said the vet. And he drew a line with the chalk, diagonally across the horse's forehead: from the base of the left ear, more or less towards the right eye. Then he drew another line, diagonally the other way. The horse stood still.

'You never want to go lower than this,' said the vet, pointing to where the lines cut. The orderly moved forward holding something, a sort of tube, which he put against the intersection of lines on the horse's forehead. The horse still stared in front of it.

Someone said: 'The old hammer type.' Simon stiffened. But he was ready to see the horse stagger, desperately trying to stand, and the death agony. The orderly's hand fell, he struck the tube and there was a small report.

The horse's knees gave way at once, so instantaneously that the eye could hardly mark its fall, and so silently that Simon might have been watching it through binoculars. It only stiffened and relaxed its legs once. The suddenness and silence of its death defeated his preparations to be unmoved.

'Now the jugular vein,' said the vet. He had a knife, and inserted it about half way down the horse's neck, so as not to spoil the skin, he said. The blood poured out exactly in the manner of water from a burst drain. The vet stood in blood, with blood running all round him, and blood jetting up over his hand. He held his hand in the incision and said casually: 'Take particular note of the colour.' It was almost black, very warm and thick.

At this point another man arrived, whose business it was to cut the horse up and take it away. First the vet was to explain the nature of the horse's insides. The man wore filthy sacking tied to him, covered with old blood. Simon noticed that the horse's face still had the same expression, though the eyes were already glazed; he felt that even now it was consciously assisting the demonstration.

The man took his knife, and drew a line with it along the exact centre of the underneath of the horse. His precision and the sharpness of his knife were uncomfortable to watch. The skin fell apart behind the knife, the vet talked on, and presently the horse lay stretched out into a diagram, to which the vet pointed as he spoke. The colours were brilliant, but not wholesome, and now a faint sweet sickly smell came from the horse. It occurred to Simon that the whole atmosphere was that of a ritual sacrifice; the vet, intoning what he had said so often before, the other man working in a scrupulous sequence, and the horse, the central figure of the ceremony, invested with the dignity due to a chosen victim. From this came the impression that the dead horse was taking a pride in its own dissection.

'The horse has a small stomach,' said the vet. 'Look!' And he flapped the stomach in front of him, like an apron. The stench was unbelievable. Simon began at last to feel sick; his hand searched frantically for his pipe, but it was not in his pocket. He looked firmly at the wreck of the horse, the crowd of spectators,

some craning their necks for a better view. The horrible casual-
ness of the vet's voice grew more and more apparent; the voice
itself increased in volume; the faces merged and disintegrated,
the wreck of the horse lay in a flurry of colours, the stench
cemented them into one chaos. He knew it was useless. His one
thought, as he felt himself falling, was that he had let the horse
down.

The Little Red Mouth

The flashes of the six pounders and of the big tanks firing their
seventy-fives impinged on the eternal glare of the sunlight,
infinitesimal moments of brightness like the scratches which
show when an old film is being projected. The boom floated
across through the shimmery air, arriving late in my right ear. In
my left ear George's voice said: 'King 3, bloody good shooting,
you're making them sit up. Keep on chucking them. Off.' His
words were a little distorted and uncomfortably loud; I took off
the left ear-phone as well and let the whole apparatus dangle
round my neck. From one of the dots on the horizon a long
straight column of black-smoke stood up, leaning a little to the
left, expanding at the top. Grey smudges showed where the
seventy-fives were falling short.

I picked up the jack-knife and carved another section of yellow
cheese out of the tin on top of the wireless set. As I began to
munch it, taking alternate bites at one of the biscuits I had laid out
beside my field-glasses and Luger on the flat roof of the turret, I
looked down into the gloom of the fighting chamber; at the faint
gleam on the breech of the two pounder, the little staircase of
cartridges climbing up to the feed slide of the machine-gun. The
gunner was reading a Wild West magazine: the driver's back
hunched forward, as he wrote a letter home on his knee; the
operator, dozing. We hadn't moved for an hour; the enemy out of
range of my obsolete gun, all the targets located — an hour of
nothing to do. I thought: 'I'll have to restart the engine or the
wireless will go dead. Spare dags need recharging anyway.' A
quarter of an hour ago I had finished 'National Velvet.' There
were no more Penguins left in the tank — only the Oxford Book of
French Verse. I opened it at random and read:

Sui-je, sui-je, suis-je belle?
Il me semble, a mon avis
que j'ai bon front et doulz viz

et la bouche vermeillette:

Dittes moy se je suis belle

and my eye fluttered down to the name, Eustache Deschamps, 1340–1410. But it made me think of Sylvie, looking up out of the corner of her black eyes, under the long Syrian lashes, saying: 'Je suis jolie, hein? Dis-moi, j'ai un joli corps?' in the very tone of voice of the poem. Et la bouche vermeillette, (Oui, c'est du Max Factor. J'en ai trouvé deux boîtes, mais deux boîtes seulment à Rivoli. Et tu sais combien j'avais à payer?) Now, at half past twelve, Sylvie is probably on the beach at Stanley with that sub-lieutenant from Mosquito. 'Nuts 5,' said the earphones. I'm awake, I'm awake. 'Nuts 5, go forward on the left, see how near you can get to the ridge. Look out for 88s. Don't swan too much. Off.' I spoke into the white rubber end of the microphone and heard the driver grinding his gears. Through the glasses, with my mind still half-occupied in Alexandria, I had already seen the little dots, with the degree-scale of the binocular lens super-imposed on them, growing smaller, receding — except three, from all of which smoke grew upwards into the dead still air.

Moving forward, oozing over the scrubby, undulating desert, my mind was still saying over, you know how a phrase can recur in your head for hours, till you forget how it came there: 'et la bouche vermeillette'. I wasn't thinking of it. I was thinking: 'Ought to go back for petrol soon. There may be a sniper in that derelict, like the one that got poor whatsisname, Sam's gunner, in the back of the neck yesterday. There may be snipers in these weapon pits.' I looked over the edge of the tank into as many weapon pits as possible. In one, away to the right, there seemed to be something more than the usual litter of packs, mess-tins, ammunition and letters. 'Driver, right. Steady' I said. 'Slow down. Halt.' I was looking down into the pit.

It was like a carefully posed waxwork. He lay propped against one end of the pit, with his neck stretched back, mouth open, dust on his tongue. Eyes open, dulled with dust; and the face, yellowish with dust, a doll's or an effigy's. He had a woollen cap on his head. The blood on his shirt was brown, hardened until the cloth was cardboard: he had opened his haversack and taken out towels to wrap round his legs against the flies. But the blood had soaked through the towels and the flies had defeated him. A crowd of flies covered him: there were black congregations of them wherever the patches of blood were, and they were crawl-ing on his face in ones and twos. His left hand was raised, supported in the air apparently by rigor mortis, the fingers crooked as though taking hold. It was this seeming to be arrested in motion, which made the pose so vivid. The right hand clutched together a corner of the towel, as if he had seized it that moment, when a wave of pain washed over him. Pain, a climax or orgasm of pain, was expressed in his face and attitude as I would not have believed a motionless body and countenance could express it. It is not too much to say his position was a cry of pain.

I looked at him, trembling with horror, stunned into involuntary speech, saying over and over again, in an audible whisper: 'et la bouche vermeillette.'

Beni Yusef, 1943

Giuseppe

Giuseppe was a parachutist. That is, he was trained as a parachutist; he learned to unpack and handle the weapons and equipment, he made the jumps. The whole of Folgore — 'the Division which will fall like mountain eagles with immaculate and beautiful heroism upon the enemy', Giuseppe's Colonel had said in his speech at the Foundation of Rome parade — the whole of Folgore had made the jumps. But they were betrayed by the Germans. The Germans (who could not think in terms of mountain eagles) had betrayed the destiny of Folgore. Folgore were sent to fight as ordinary infantry, and as ordinary infantry, singing their songs, leaping upon their parapets with bravado, and hurling their little red grenades into the very mouths of the British infantry, they had perished 'with immaculate and beautiful heroism.' Giuseppe had escaped.

He had found a motor cycle, and being luckily near the coast road, had caught up with the retreating army and attached himself to the Young Fascists, who had not yet seen action. Since then he had had many occupations and some changes of formation along the hundreds of miles of thirst and dejection — from Mersa to Tobruck, Tobruck to Benghazi and the green country, the trees filtering the sunlight gratefully, the white bungalows of the colonists. Passing through the plains strewn with blue flowers, to Sirte and Nufilia, Giuseppe was one of those who scrawled W IL DUCE and RITORNEREMO on the cracked white plaster of walls. But Tripoli had fallen, and still Giuseppe had gone back, back, with the Italians; dirty, covered with lice and ticks, remembering the betrayal of the mountain eagles, hating the Germans more than the English, tired of the war. He had become, in the end, viciously disposed towards everybody. And when, in the last fight for Tunisia, his formation were assigned to the defence of a great height in the Matmata hills, with the crowded walls of an Arab village built like a castle on its summit, Giuseppe was no more good as a soldier: jumpy, he was, sure of death, but not knowing when it would come.

Now he lay in a stone pit, blasted out of the mountain side by engineers. In the daytime it was not safe to move out of the pit; accordingly it stank and the walls moved with flies. The two others who shared the pit with him were trying to sleep, curled on the floor of it, sprawling among a mass of old magazines, letters, empty tins, broken Chianti bottles in their straw jackets. The empty cases of the Breda cartridges littered the floor round Giuseppe's feet: they had been fired in repelling the last attack. It was Giuseppe's turn on the gun. In the last attack they had thrown back the brown savages, New Zealanders, the officer had said when he visited the post afterwards. Miore, or some such name. Giuseppe and his comrades did not care, only that they had thrown them back. The shelling had seemed to split the mountain, and then here were these Miore, climbing like goats, hurling grenades into the posts, right on top of them with their flat noses and queer shouts. One of them had almost reached this post, halfway up the steep flank of the mountain. His body, stiff and dusty, with the blood congealed about the smashed eye, lay a yard or two down the slope, where it had caught on a toe of rock. Theoretically, Giuseppe thought, it was a good thing to have him there, to distract the flies a little from the men in the post. But here were the flies, still tearing away with their little telescopic suckers at the sores on his hand. Down the slope, he could hear a wounded man moaning, lying out in the full sun.

There were others further down, and scattered about among the fig-trees at the base of the mountain. Some dead. Some wounded. Earlier in his spell of duty, Giuseppe had seen a movement down there, and belted off a few rounds, without being able to see the result. Then the shelling had begun again. Now it was a lull.

Suddenly, with a pang of terror, he saw men moving down at the bottom of the slope, where the posts had been driven in, and their crews killed or captured. But he saw it was only the movement of two men, who had crawled up and were trying to drag away some of the wounded down a small wadi that ran to the edge of the fig-trees. They must have taken some risks to get *there*, he thought. Anyway, they've taken their last risk now. He sprayed bullets at them, not troubling to hold the bucking gun firmly, and saw them suddenly throw their arms and legs about like marionettes whose string is jerked too hard. Later he saw a few men running and dodging among the fig-trees. Evidently they had had enough. He fired at them too, but did not observe any hits. The afternoon dragged into evening and darkness.

An hour before dawn, after a cold night, and stiff with their cramped quarters, they were roused by an officer on rounds, and stood to, watching the sky lightening over the vast plain which their position commanded, on which the roads, the squares of fields, and the dark rough masses of trees stretched away for mile upon mile. The attack came half an hour or so afterwards. There was no preliminary shelling. They heard the tanks somewhere at the foot of the hill, coming right up to the beginning of the slope. They must be mad, to attack a mountain with tanks. But the tanks withdrew, when they had smashed a way through the cactus hedges, and the infantry poured through the gaps. Giuseppe heard and recognised their war cries. In the dim light he could see them coming up through the posts below him. There was a continual rattle of small arms fire, punctuated by the boom of grenade explosions echoing in defiles and splits in the rock. Giuseppe's nerve gave way. He left his position and scrambled sideways in panic across the hill. Sometimes he fell and rolled almost down among the combatants, but he made his way, driven by a subconscious resolve to get to the side of the mountain away from the enemy, to the western slope; where, on a table of rock somewhat below the level he had left, were a few scattered Arab houses, to which a sort of track led up from the valley. Already they were fighting there. He saw two Italian soldiers come out to surrender in the increasing light, to be shot in the stomach before they could open their mouths or raise their hands, by a Maori with a tommy-gun. Giuseppe crawled, palpitating, under the wreck of a Spa lorry while he heard the terrifying noises of the fight dying away. Once a bullet smashed through the woodwork above him, and another whined away from a rock a yard or two off, but for the moment, he was safe. He crawled out a little way, after half-an-hour, to see if he could escape. There was no one alive in the area where he was.

Looking down he saw the immense side of the mountain

sloping away to the fields and the outskirts of the shell-torn
European town. Looking up, he saw the mountain tower against
the rosy dawn sky. He heard a scream from somewhere high
above him, a human scream approaching rapidly like the scream
of a shell; and saw the body of a man fly out, black against the sky
for a moment, making the motions of a swimmer, and screaming.
The man fell with a short noise of impact on the hard ground,
doubled up in an impossible position. Now the bodies of live men
began to hurtle down, one after another. Most of them screamed.
After a quarter of an hour, the falling of men stopped as a
hailstorm stops, suddenly. In the early morning sunlight of a
Tunisian winter day, Giuseppe saw the single figure of a Maori
standing, high up, outlined against the sky. He was shouting
down a message to the dead men. 'That's what you bastards get
for machine gunning our wounded,' he yelled, in a voice cracked
with fury and exhaustion. Giuseppe did not understand the
English words.

❧

Douglas spent much of his Christmas leave 1943/1944
gathering his poems for the collection Tambimuttu had
proposed. Tambimuttu already had the MS of *Alamein to
Zem Zem*, referred to by Douglas as 'the Diary' because of
the book in which it was written. How exactly to make best
use of its narrative material, preoccupied his thinking during
the next weeks. The 'difficulties' he refers to are no doubt
those of libel, military censorship and the responses of the
people he portrayed.

❧

2 [*January 1944*]   *Feock, Cornwall*

Dear Tambi, I had a shot at finding you when I was in town on the
31st, but failed to find even the Diary, which I wanted to take
away . . . I hope you aren't losing it or showing it to anyone at all
official. I have collected nearly 80 poems, and discovered the
negatives of some of the photographs, though not as yet of the
dead men.

I have been thinking over the idea of a book containing prose,
verse, photographs and drawings, and I think the best arrangement would be to produce a fairly small volume, called something like Landscape with figures, or Figures on a battlefield,
with an oddish jacket. [annotated sketch follows]

Inside the book 10 prose pieces taken from the diary, dealing with actual scenes, and cutting out, for the moment, the bits of character study etc., which would cut out a lot of my difficulties: the idea being entirely to give a vivid picture, more than an account. 10 photographs, which need not necessarily be selected from mine — although at least some of mine would do (I can get the dead men negatives). 10 poems, all to do with the battlefields between Alamein and Tunisia, possibly one or two letters from the battlefield to my mother or anyone else, and 10 drawings. There might be a sort of 'leave' section of the book clearing out of the battlefield back to Cairo, which could include Behaviour of Fish in an Egyptian teagarden, and an excellent photograph of the teagarden which I happen to have, and a description of being wounded, in hospital, and on leave.

This may sound very disjointed, but I think my careful arrangement could be more of a unity than simply poems and a straightforward account. If it seemed too much you could cut out the drawings.

It would need some sort of a preface, which I could write. That's all at the moment. If you cared to produce the big mass of poems in an ordinary verse volume you could still do that. If so I want to write a sort of essay at the beginning. The poems divide into School and Oxford, Army at home and in Palestine, and poems about Cairo and the battlefield. The styles of these 3 groups are so different that they would have to be separated and a little written about each Division in the preface.

I shall be in town two days about the 6th and 7th or 7th and 8th, and should like to see you if possible (let's say the 7th) as it may be my last chance for some time. Also, I want the book (Diary) back when I go back to the regiment, on the 8th or 9th. So if you can't see me, please give the Diary to Betty Jesse and I'll ask for her and get it (also your comments, if you don't see me). I'll ring up as soon as I get to town and try to make a definite appointment with you. I am writing this from Porthgwidden, Feock, Cornwall. My address at the Regiment, is

Cpt. K. C. Douglas
Notts SR Yeo
Chippenham Park. North Camp
Ely
Cambs
(in case I didn't give it you before.)

When I next come I'll leave the whole bulk of poems for you and you can see if you like them. Please don't lose them if you can help it, because although I have copies of most of them they are scattered and will be hard to get at.

Hoping to see you   *Keith Douglas*

30 January [1944]   *Ely, Cambs*

Dear Tambi, I believe I am getting leave for 12 days from Monday Feby 14th. This is certainly my last leave for 3 months, possibly for a great deal longer (or for good, I suppose). It may be permissible for me to get away from Saturday to Sunday at another time — but I doubt if that'll be much good for catching you. So I shall come straight up to London on Monday and stay if necessary till Wednesday, in order to see you.

I hope by that time you'll have read over the typed version of the diary and decided what you like and dislike in it, and if you want it at all. I shall bring with me the following drawings, from which I suggest we select 10.

1) Tanks advancing up a sand track (watercolour).
2) Composition based on a Piéta, of casualty being taken out of a tank (watercolour).
3) as 2) above. (Pen drawing).
4) Face of a man burning to death (watercolour, with explanatory notes in ink).
5) Sketch of bodies and junk, with notes of ideas for a poem (pencil).
6) Shapes of derelicts (watercolour).
7) Tanks under HE fire.
8) Derelicts (watercolour).
9) Broken Trees and buildings (watercolour).
10) Tank crews cooking (pen drawing).
11) Crusader tanks moving up into battle (watercolour).
12) Men hit by anti-personnel mine (pen drawing).
13) Derelict lorry and anti-tank guns (watercolour).
14) Cairo street scene (caricatures) pen and wash.
15) Explosion of a booby trap (pen drawing).
16) Self-portrait in a steel shaving mirror (pencil).

Whatever these may seem to you to lack, as pictures, they give an accurate idea of the appearance of things, with one exception. In the case of the man burning to death I have had to retain all the features, to give the chap some expression, although of course they're expressionless, as their faces swell up like pumpkins. But I've got the effect I wanted, of pain. Or I think I have.

I may also bring you a poem or two more — and if you're interested in short stories about the Middle East I have four so far written and may have more when I come. But I don't expect you want short stories. I shall have some more of the diary — but it's all very similar.

As to the title of the book, I think it should be something more individual than Journey into Battle, which sounds like a war-correspondent's account. Here are some more suggestions although there's bags of time yet.

1. Another Part of the Battlefield.
2. The Iron Trees (this sounds as if its aping Sidney Keyes [*The Iron Laurel*, 1942], though).
3. A Man in Armour, or, Men in Armour.
4. The New Country.
5. The Iron Country.
6. Anatomy of Battle or Anatomy of a Battle.

I like 1, 6, and 5, in that order (I've been writing them down as I thought of them.) I'll do a design for a jacket if you decide on a title.

Send me a date and time, please.   *Keith Douglas*

P.S. I suppose it's with your knowledge and consent that the BBC are proposing to broadcast 'Enfidaville'?

By the end of February Douglas had a contract for a collection of poems to be called 'Bête Noire' and had been paid an advance of £10.0.0. The advance, like the contract, was soon to be in jeopardy. As his training for the invasion of the mainland of Europe quickened in pace, he awaited a decision on the narrative, with increasing impatience. In March his Colonel read the text and passed it, and Douglas sent copies to the widow of 'Flash' ('Piccadilly Jim'), and to Jocelyn Baber, a friend. Though his war poems had been appearing in the Cairo magazine *Personal Landscape*, none had appeared in English journals since 'The Trumpet' in the *T.L.S.* (26 June 1943). *Poetry (London)* had not come out for twelve months.

During his visits to London Douglas had seen little of Tambimuttu's literary circle, but had struck up an increasingly close friendship with his assistant at *Poetry (London)*, Betty Jesse. At the start of March he heard from her that there was not yet any decision on 'the Diary'.

◆

To BETTY JESSE (extract)
March 1944

. . . I suppose you'll get someone to read it sometime: after all, I suppose they do read everything that's submitted sooner or later. Anyway it's sweet of you to try. If you finally come to the conclusion that it's no use trying, please send it back, and I'll scrap it.

To BETTY JESSE (extract)
10 March 1944

About Tambi, is it any good my saying will he either make up his mind or send it back because someone else wants it? I am writing a letter to this effect and I'll put it in this one. If you think it's a good thing, give it him. If not, tear it up. Needless to say I don't want it back and no one else wants it, though I dare say I could persuade Faber's, who view me with a kindly eye (Uncle Eliot's) or Gollancz.

[*?10 March 1944*]

Dear Tambi, I don't know if you want the Diary to publish or not. But will you make up your mind by the 24th of March, and let me know by then, because if you don't want it or if I don't hear by that date I shall submit it to someone else *on* the 24th, who seems interested in it. I can't afford to wait because of military engagements which might be the end of me — so that date is final.
    Yours   *Keith*

13 March 1944   *Poetry (London)*

Dear Keith, Tambi is going to publish your diary. Can you please get it ready for publication as soon as possible?
    He is going to use 7 or 8 of your paintings and I am enclosing two — PIETA and MEN HIT BY ANTI PERSONNEL MINE, and he asks if you could possibly re-draw these if you have time.

He is intending to use some of your war poems with the diary, and he suggests that the title should be something simple like WAR DIARY: THE TUNISIAN CAMPAIGN WITH POEMS AND DRAWINGS BY KEITH DOUGLAS.

We are anxious to print as soon as possible, so perhaps you could let me have an early word as to when the manuscript will be ready.

Yours sincerely   *Betty Jesse*

[*March 1944*]   *Nuffield House SW1*

Dear Tambi, I've had the agreement from Betty. I don't agree about the £10 for various reasons. I've signed my part of the 2nd agreement and Dorothy Sauter has signed yours, and you *have*, therefore agreed to publish two books. Now if you could use the majority of my poems in the War Diary, I wouldn't mind you amalgamating the two — although I still don't see why *I* should be punished, by a fine of £10, because *you* have changed your mind. Do you think its fair, yourself? Secondly out of the 70–80 poems I've submitted to you for a book of poems (which you definitely asked me for) you *can* only use about 15 with the War Diary, so that the others don't get published at all. Now if I had not severed or allowed to drop, all connections with T.S. Eliot and with Fabers, I could probably have got those poems published by them. Now I don't suppose I'll get them published at all, unless you stand by your agreement. Of course I don't give a damn how *long* you take to publish the poems, within reason: publish the Diary first and the poems later (when they'll sell better, I think, as a result of people having read the diary). Also I hear you like the Bête Noire cover drawing and so do I; and it seems a pity not to use it.

To go back to the agreement — you are paying me only for my MS and you are using a lot of illustrations. That's OK. I submitted them with the MS, as part of it. But the fact remains that if you had got anyone else to illustrate it you'd have had to pay him extra, above the advance royalties you're paying me. So it seems a bit hard to *deduct* £10, doesn't it?

Finally, merely from the point of view of £10 more, or less, as you know I owe my mother about £40 and she is quite broke, and so I must pay it. This doesn't leave me a lot over, and there are a lot of rather expensive things — e.g. a warm and waterproof coat, and a good sleeping bag, which I shall be needing for the next battle and which the British Government does not supply me with. So the £10 in itself makes quite a lot of difference.

So I suggest —

1) That deducting £10 is not very fair — Betty agrees with me, I believe.
2) That you don't deduct it.
3) That you publish the diary first and wait a bit and then
4) Publish Bête Noire — by which time I can let you have about 20 more poems — I already have 5 or 6.

After all — you have signed agreements to publish two separate MSS — and I think in the end you'll be glad if you do publish both.

Now — Page 3. Points about the Diary

1) I have completed it up to my arrival in hospital.

   This only makes it about 25 pp of type longer than it was, and does not include a description of my stay in hospital, or of the very small piece of the Tunisian campaign which I saw. I could go on, but it is a natural whole as it stands, and I think would be spoilt by a continuation. I have some more drawings to go in it. (Pen ones).

2) *Title* — call it

   A Journal of some Desert Battles

   or A Journal of Desert Battles

   or A Journal of the battles from Alamein to Zem Zem

      with poems and drawings

      by

      Keith Douglas

3) I could write a last chapter, an account of the final surrender of the German armies in Tunisia — this would be another 10 to 15 pages, and ought to be inserted last, so that you have

     — one poem

       prologue

     — the main diary

       epilogue

     — the poems

     — Description of the end in Tunisia.

When I let you have the final MS will you —

1) Let PL Solicitors look it over ref. libel.
2) get it retyped and charge it to me out of the 2nd £30.

Sorry this is so long.

   Yours *Keith*

P.S. Militarily, things begin to move, for me, very soon now, so once you've got this MS I may be fairly busy.

26 [March 1944]   *Notts SR Yeo APO England*

Dear Betty, You seem to be receiving a lot of communications from me, none of them very interesting — although anyone in the office who recognizes my writing will be supposing I write you 'long marvellous letters' every day. Well, this one begins with business, too. I sent you a receipt for the £30. It doesn't look much like a receipt to me, and I had to pull the 2d stamp off a postcard: however my squadron clerk, who is something in the city in civvy street says it is OK. If you look carefully at the stamp you'll find the signature continues across it, although if you lift it up you'll find another signature underneath.

Secondly, a few points about the Diary which have cropped up in my mind.

1) A censor may raise objections to the detailed description of wireless procedure during battle — giving away code names etc. It might be as well — since censors are not only ignorant but dimwitted *and* in a hell of a hurry — to mention that this procedure has been completely cancelled and is never used — and anyway the enemy knew all about it, because we captured an interception officer who explained all our own codes to us. The main point is that such a procedure no longer exists.

2) *The Title* — I think we said

A Journal of the Battles from

Alamein to Zem Zem

Would it make a more arresting title from the bookstall point of view to call it

Alamein — Zem Zem

A Journal of some desert battles

with

poems and drawings

in that order. Whether any play could be made with the fact that the initials make it A–Z I don't know. As you probably saw, inside the cover I've called the beginning and the ending bits A and Z anyway to avoid the words Prologue and epilogue. You could probably get rid of the hyphen and imply it in the lay-out of the words e.g. [Sketch of what K.D. suggests] or something, like travelling labels (though not travelling label lettering, I hope). I am enclosing another poem ['Mersa'] which is relevant to the diary.

[Added upside-down at foot of this letter:]
Will you look up SKELETAL in a dictionary (I haven't one) and find out if it exists and means like a skeleton. If not, alter Skeletal in MERSA to Skeleton. And please ensure Tambi has a copy of a poem CAIRO JAG beginning Shall I get drunk or cut myself a piece of cake and that he uses it? Thanks.

4 April 1944   *Notts SR Yeo APO England*

Dear Tambi, Here are 2 new poems ['On a Return from Egypt' and 'Egyptian Sentry . . .'] and another copy of the one I sent off yesterday, because I don't trust the Army Post Office an inch. If there are variations between the 2 versions of L'Autobus, use whichever you prefer.
    Yours   *Keith*

On 6 April 1944 the regiment left Chippenham for Sway, where they prepared for the Normandy landings in a top security camp, prohibited to civilians.

[March/April 1944]   *Notts SR Yeo APO England*

Dear Edmund, I hoped I might hear an address from you after I got back, as I know you've left Merton. I'm going to send this to Jean who seems to see you from time to time. I'm afraid even now this is a short letter. As you will see from my cryptic address I've been fattened up for more slaughter and am simply waiting for it to start. Nicholson & Watson have paid the £60 and 10% on any further sales for my diary of the battles from Alamein to Zem Zem with poems and illustrations and a measley £10 (+10%) for a book of poems called Bête Noire at the moment, which, with my cover and illustrations, will probably appear later. I am not much perturbed at the thought of never seeing England again, because a country which can allow her army to be used to the last gasp and paid like skivvies isn't worth fighting for. For me, it is simply a case of fighting *against* the Nazi regime. After that, unless there is a revolution in England, I hope to depart for sunnier and less hypocritical climates.

I wish you good luck with your new ménage.   *Keith*

To JOCELYN BABER
28 May 1944

Thank you a lot for your letter and the review of my book, which was most interesting, particularly the criticisms.

To answer these — since I never go down without a fight —

(1) Two identical descriptions of Sam. I have left these in, because, until you mentioned it, no one had carped at them, and although I had realised there was a certain amount of tautology, I did not think the two descriptions were so identical as all that.

(2) The change of names was due to the fact that they sent the carbon copies of the first part of the book — I had meanwhile corrected the original typescript. The second part of the book I submitted with corrected names so the carbon copy was correct. Anyway, that one *is* taken care of.

(3) Night at Milena's. You mind because it possibly seems to drag down the level of tragedy suggested by the charm round Norman's neck, and of a fine acceptance of this on my part — and that is, I suppose, because you sense a sort of crawling round behind Norman's back in my conduct, and a general atmosphere of dubious intrigue. You want 'selectivity' again — a suppression of something ugly but true. (Personally, I don't think of it as ugly but then I know why we embraced again). This is all bound up with the question of allowing the sergeant in on it. Well, as you accuse yourself over this, let me only say you merit the accusation thoroughly. This bit — i.e. Milena — I have altered, but not deleted. It is far too much intertwined with the whole story, to cut out. There is no fusty scent except what lingers from an incident which does not come in to the story — but which led to the triangular situation. And for *that* fusty scent Norman is responsible, not I.

(4) Loot — dogmess etc.

I have discussed this with several people and the dogmess *definitely* stands. Loot is one of the most important things — and it is the thing that makes all that exhilaration in fighting. And believe it or not, our utmost thought at the end of the battle was loot. By that you must not understand — as I believe you do — pillaging or corpse robbing. But simply rummaging in the glorious bran tub provided by any battlefield. One's requirements and desires in any case were pretty basic. In fact, it's a picture of a dogmess; so you can't cut the dogmess out — and I am afraid I refuse to cut it out to suit the connoisseur sensibilities of yourself, Lavender and Stella or for mother, whose objections are based on her incorrigible sentimentality . . . . (I'm not sure the instinct for selectivity isn't based on sentimentality anyhow). Perhaps you will get to like it — like —

   O ces voix d'enfants chantant dans la coupole

which so jarred on George Moore's ear at first and finally became a favourite line of his. We'll see —   [Keith]

On 6 June he sailed for Normandy. Three days later, near St Pierre, he was killed.

28 June 1944   67 Pembury Rd, Tonbridge

Dear Mrs Douglas, Your letter reaches me only by this afternoon's post. I also heard today from Oxford in answer to my inquiry there — for there seemed just a hope that the casualty list (which I did not see) had been misreported. I must say at once that your letter is one of the most courageous I have ever read and that Keith would have said it was exactly what he wished. But I am terribly sorry at your losing him; and for my own small part in his story I hate to think that it is cut short thus. No doubt all human affairs are 'inevitable', but I cannot rest from the doubt when such wars largely of an origin in contending ambitions are worked out in the sufferings of those who did not share those.

   And I thought that Keith had quite done enough of active service, seeing that it is required of his generation; but war does not take any account of *that*.

   It is something that, as you say, he had made vigorous and enterprising use of his time, and already achieved a place among the young poets and leading spirits. I would also say, among Old Blues who will be present to the imagination of aftercomers at our old school, and kindle fresh endeavours among them — a great thing you will agree. To me it seems *most* desirable that a volume of his verse, with some account of him and some examples of his work as an artist, should be published. You speak of some such project, and maybe I shall hear if one of his contemporaries is ready to edit it — it needs the whole collection of his papers as a start. Anything that I can do in respect of the book on Alamein I will, and shall await a sight of the proofs whenever you can send them. My expectations of this record are high; he saw things with a remarkable keenness.

I did not see him when he last visited Oxford, alas, through my own wanderings and changes; but I didn't dream it would be long before he was with us all again, out of the Army and back to his own plans and works. I was always fond of him and flattered myself that he treated my 'advice' kindly and reflectively; and he is in a manner present in this place as I write, cheerful and disputatious and affectionate. I am *very* glad you have his friend [John Bethell-Fox] so near you, and it must be more than coincidence if I know K. C. D.

Yours sincerely   *E. Blunden*

Sources

The bulk of Douglas's MSS are in the British Library (*BL*). Acquired at different times they have various numbers. Other MSS together with Douglas's books, photographs and memorabilia are in the Brotherton Collection at Leeds University (*Brotherton*). All Douglas's side to the correspondence with Blunden is in the Blunden Papers at the Harry Ransom Humanities Research Center, The University of Texas at Austin. Sources for other letters are as follows:

from Blunden to Douglas and Mrs Douglas: *BL* Add Ms 56356
from Blunden to T. S. Eliot: in the possession of Mrs T. S. Eliot
from Douglas to T. S. Eliot: *BL* 60587
from T. S. Eliot to Douglas: *BL* 56356, reprinted *TLS* 2 July 1970
from Douglas to J. C. Hall: in the possession of J. C. Hall except for letter of [17 Oct. 1941], *BL* Add Ms 53773
from J. C. Hall to Mrs Douglas: *BL* Add Ms 56356
from Douglas to M. J. Tambimuttu and Betty Jesse of 'Poetry (London)': *BL* Add Mss 53773, 60587
from Tambimuttu and Betty Jesse to Douglas: *BL* Add Ms 56356
from Douglas to Jocelyn Baber: *BL* Add Ms 56356

Later versions of all the poems included in letters are in *The Complete Poems of Keith Douglas* (O.U.P. 1978), except for 'Negative Information', 'Adams', 'The 2 Virtues' and 'Aristocrats', which are as printed here. The most significant revision is to 'The Sniper' which, as 'How to Kill', reads (line 18): 'How easy it is to make a ghost' (*CP* p. 112). 'For E.B.' is uncollected.

For *Alamein to Zem Zem*, see below.

Other sources:

'An Untitled Autobiographical Story': *Brotherton*
from 'An Unfinished Autobiographical Fragment': *BL* Add Ms 56359L

'Strange Gardener': (see *CP* p. 5) *BL* Add Ms 59834
'Reading': *BL* Add Ms 59834
'On Getting to know a poet': *BL* Add Ms 59834
'Words': *BL* Add Ms 60586
Augury: ed. K. C. Douglas and A. M. Hardie, (Blackwell, Oxford 1940)
'The Butterflies': *Citadel* (Cairo) March 1943, pp. 32–4
'Poets in This War': *TLS* 23 April 1971, p. 478 (Ms in *BL*)
'A Dead Gunner': (see 'Vergissmeinnicht' *CP* p.111) *Brotherton*
'Death of a Horse': *Lilliput*, July 1944 pp. 51–2
'The Little Red Mouth': *Stand* (Newcastle upon Tyne) vol. XI no. 2, (1970) pp. 9–11 (MS in *BL*)
'Giuseppe': *BL* Add Ms 56357

Alamein to Zem Zem:

'Fragment on the first page of an Italian exercise book' (*BL* Add Ms 60586) appears to pre-date the complete surviving MS of *Alamein*, 'the Diary' (*BL* Add Ms 53774) and could well be the very start of the narrative's composition. A fragment of 'Aristocrats' also in the exercise book would suggest a date after late April 1943. One who was with Douglas at El Ballah, however, recalls Douglas composing the narrative there: see, 'A Soldier's Story', *PN Review* Spring 1985.

The abandoned draft, revising part of *Alamein to Zem Zem* (*BL* Add Ms 60586; I will refer to it as the 'fragment') was made later than the corresponding part of 'the Diary', incorporating additions noted in the margins of that MS. The fragment, a typescript, was probably made around September 1943. Douglas had no time for full-scale revisions in England in 1944 and submitted 'the Diary' version to Tambimuttu. A typescript was made from it, and submitted to the printer for publication in December 1946. Douglas supervised that typescript which must have included numerous revisions: further changes were made to it post-humously, for reasons of military censorship, libel etc. The 1946 text remains the basis of the latest edition (O.U.P. 1979).

The fragment, which is closer to 'the Diary' than to the pub-lished text reveals Douglas's thinking before his own later thoughts and those of others had intervened. The character studies are blunter and far less tempered, particularly those of 'Andrew', 'Mudie' and 'Evan', which are in sufficiently crude form for me to have retained the pseudonyms (the real names of others are restored). The description of the Colonel, for example, here given his true nickname 'Flash', is far more forthright and shows him, admirably, to have connived in Douglas's unofficial return, when confronted with the *fait accompli:* 'I think a policy of Masterly Inactivity is indicated. . .'. Douglas's later omission of this could well have stemmed from care for the Colonel's official reputation; similarly, his toning down of the description of the confusion of their dawn entry into the battlefield might have arisen from his awareness that the book had to pass military censorship. That description, however, might also have been altered so as to remove some of his niggling on about 'Andrew'. It is impossible finally to distinguish the potential motives. What is not in doubt is the fragment's more direct presentation of Douglas's outlook: his capacity for severe criticism which included a tendency to go on about people; his desire, despite this, to be wholly just.

Douglas's responses to his situation are also more directly portrayed in the fragment. Where in the published text he writes of being afraid that his idea of running back to the regiment would seem absurd to those he encountered, in the fragment he writes of a fear that his plan would be laughed at and his confidence in it destroyed. The fragment spells out a little more specifically his response to the news of the deaths which preceded his arrival, and he closes his first section with the observation, later omitted: 'There lay so many strange scenes, the answers to so many questions.' Such changes are part of a tidying up and purposeful directing of his material which makes the published version more effective in style, but they are also a, wholly justifiable, tidying up of his character. In the fragment we find his simple fancy at work in describing the great bulk of a Grant tank as 'looking like a castle in the moonlight', the shells sounding like 'gigantic invisible trains'. His later focusing on the most significant detail leads him to write of the tanks crouching 'still, but alive, like toads'. In the fragment a less effective but more telling detail received emphasis: the tanks crouch 'cold-bloodedly alive, like toads'.

A couple of points of literary interest emerge from the fragment; one of them slight, the other of great importance. The fragment proves that the poem 'based on the idea of the ominous pregnancy of the moon which at the beginning of battle was in its first quarter' was in fact 'The Offensive'. More revealingly, a reference there to Stephen Crane, later omitted, directly helps our understanding of the narrative's literary ancestry. To place the passage in which this reference occurs beside the same part of the published text is to see how much closer to Douglas the fragment brings us. If the later text's compression and swiftness, derived from the fragment's more ruminative material, finely prove Douglas's skill as a writer, the more leisurely and loose association of ideas in the fragment allows us to see more of himself. The *Alamein* piece is given first; that from the fragment, second:

> Silence is a strange thing to us who live: we desire it, we fear it, we worship it, we hate it. There is a divinity about cats, as long as they are silent: the silence of swans gives them an air of legend. The most impressive thing about the dead is their triumphant silence, proof against anything in the world.

> Silence is a strange thing to us who are alive. We desire it, fear, worship, and hate it. If cats were worshipped, it was surely for their silence; swans are majestic and legendary creatures because of their silence and silent movements. And Stephen Crane speaks of a dead man on a battlefield who had the air of having the answer to life. It is the silence of the dead that gives them this air; their triumphant silence, proof against any questioner in the world.